What the Names in the Bible Mean

JOSEPH BAHRIBEK

WHAT THE NAMES IN THE BIBLE MEAN

iUniverse books may be ordered through booksellers or by contacting:

iUniverse
1663 Liberty Drive
Bloomington, IN 47403
www.iuniverse.com
1-800-Authors (1-800-288-4677)

Because of the dynamic nature of the Internet, any web addresses or links contained in this book may have changed since publication and may no longer be valid. The views expressed in this work are solely those of the author and do not necessarily reflect the views of the publisher, and the publisher hereby disclaims any responsibility for them.

Any people depicted in stock imagery provided by Getty Images are models, and such images are being used for illustrative purposes only. Certain stock imagery © Getty Images.

ISBN: 978-1-5320-9924-3 (sc)
ISBN: 978-1-5320-9925-0 (e)

Library of Congress Control Number: 2020909160

Print information available on the last page.

iUniverse rev. date: 03/04/2021

Introduction

My book is to let you know about the name in the Bible & also your name. This book is comprehensive guide to all the name proper attributed to individual people in the Bible. The people listed here are historical human being. Wonderd how man name in Bible as such it genealogy does not list entries to titles. The people listed here are historical human being. In this book is also genealogy dictionary of name of Bible from where they came and also the name of places.

J.E.B.

Aaron.	Aaron a son of Amram and Jochebed of the tribe of Levi, born in Egypt in 1597 B.C.E. Levi was Aaron graeat-grandfather. (Ex 6:13.16-20 Miriam was his elder sister, and Moses was younger brother by three years. (Ex. 2:1-4; 7:7) Aaron marrid Elisheba, daughter of Amminadab and had four sons, Nadab, Abihu, Eleazar and Ithmar (Ex. 6:23). He died in 1474 B.C.
ABaddon.	Meaning Destrction of Revelation 9:11 this Hebrew word is translitrad into the English.
ABBA.	Abba the word Abba in Aramic correspond to emphatic or definte from of av in Hebrew meaning the father.
ABDA.	Servant.
Abdeel.	Servant of God.
Abdi.	Shortend from of Abdial.
Abdiel.	Servant of God.
Abednego.	Probably servant of Nebo a Babylonian god the nam given to Azariah one of the youths of Jewish royalty or nobility taken captive by Nebuchadnezzar in 617 B.C.
Abel.	Abel the second son of Adam and the younger brother of their firstborn son, Cain. Ge. 4:2. Abel had sisters. The names are not mention in Old Testaments in (Ge.).

Abiasaph.	Abiasaph. My father has gatered on of three son of Korah the Levite, and a descendant of Kohath. Ex. 6:16-24.
Abiathar.	Father of Excellence; Faher of more than Enough. Overflow. A son of High prest Ahimelech of tribe of Live.
Abida.	Father has known me Abida was a son of Midian and a grandson of Abraham by his wife Keturah. He had four brothers named Ephah, Epher, Hanoch and Eldaad. Ge. 25:1,2,4.
Abidan.	My father has judged.
Abiel.	My father is God. A son of Zeror, and descendent of Bechohath and Aphiah, of the tribe of Benjamin.
AbiEzer.	My father is helper. One of sons of Gilead the grandson of Manasseh.
Abihail.	My father is vital energy. The nam three men and two women in the Old Testament. A man of tribe of Live & of the family or cland of Merari.
Abihu.	He is father. One of Aaron four son by his wife Elisheba brother of Nadab, Eleazar & Ithamar Ex. 6:23; 1 Ch. 6:31; 24;1 Born in Egypt. Abihu second son of Aaron.
Abihud.	Possibly father is Dignity a descendent of Benjamin. Through his first born, Bela 1 Ch; 8:1-13.

ABijah.   My father is God.

Abimael.   A descendant of Sham through Arpachshad has father was Joktan, whose brother, Peleg was an ancestor of Abraham. Ge. 10:28, Ch. 1:17-27.

ABimelech.   My father is king. Either a personal nam or an offical title of several Philistine kings.

Abinoam.   Father is pleasantness. The father of Judge Barak, & descendant of Naphtal.

Abram.   Father is High. Reubenit, the son of Eliab & brother or Dathan & Nemuel.

Abishai.   Posibly father is Exisis. The son of David's sister or half sister Zeruiah & brother of Joab & Asahel Ch. 2:15; 16.

Abishua.   Probably father is Help. Benjamite of the family of Bela. Ch. 8:1-4. The son of Phinehas & a great-great son of Aaron. He was the father of Bukki. 1 Ch. 6:4, 5, 50, 51.

Abishur.   Father is a protective. A descendant of Judh through the family line of Hezron of the hous of Jerahmeel.

Abitub.   Father is Goodness. A Benjmitie, evidently the son Shaharaim by his wife Hushim. 1 Ch. 8:8.11.

Abiud.   Possbly father is Dignity. Abiud, descendant of Zerurbbabel & an ancestor St. Joseph the father of Jesus on Earth.

Ab Ner.   Father is Lamp. Son of Ner of tribe of Benjamin, First Samuel 14:50, 51 evidently refers to Ab Ner as Uncle of Saul.

Abraham.   Father of three Nation. Father of Nation. Abraham was native of Ur.

Absalom.   Father that is God is peace. The third of six sons born to David at Hebron.

Acacia.   A tree that grow will in the wilderness.

Accad.   One of the four cities founded by Nimrod that formed the begining of his kingdom. Ge. 10:10 Accad Akkad.

Achbor.   Jerboas Jumping Rodent. The father of Baal-hanan, who listed as the seventh king of Edom. Ge. 36:38, 39. 1 Ch. 1:49.

Achish.   A Philistine king of Gath who reigned during the time of David & Solomon. He was the son of Moach or Maach, & in the superscription of Psalm 34 is called Abimeleck.

Ach Sah.   Anklet; Bengle. The daughter of Judean Spy Galeb whom he offered in marriage as who over captured the stronghold of Debri in Judah newly acquird territory. Galeb's nephew Othniel. Who evidntly became the first juge after Joshua Jg 3;9, 10.

Adah.   Shortened from of Eleadah or Adaiah. The first Lamech's two livig wives. She was the mother of Jabal and Jubal the founder of nomadic berdsman and musicians respectively. Ge. 4:19-23. A Cananite daughter of Elon the Hittite & one of Esau's wive.

Adaiah.   The Lord has decked the nameholder. Descndat of Levi's son.

Adalla.   Gershom and an ancistor of Asaph. 1 Ch. 6:39-43 on of Haman's ten sons. Es.
               9:7-10.

Adam.   Earthing man; mankind. Human-being. From roat - meaning red is blood.

Addar.   Son of Bela, a Banjamite. 1 Ch. 8:1, 3.

Adiel.   God is an ornament. The father Azmaveth. Who king David appointed to be
               over his royal treasure hous. 1 Ch. 27:25, 31.

Adin.   Pleasure-give one of the paternal head of Israel.

Adina.   From root meaning luxuriate that is get pleasure the son of Shiza.

Admatha.   From Persian, meaning unconquered one of the seven princes in the kingdom
               of Persia and Media who had access to King Ahasuerus.

Adna.   Pleasure.

Adnah.   Pleasure.

Adoni-Bezek.   Lord of Bezek.

Adonijah.   God is Lord. David fourth son, born of Haggith in He boran.

Adonikam.   My God Lord has raised Himself up that is, to help.

Adoniram.   My Lord is high. son of Abde.

Adrammelech.   Son of King Sennacherib of Assyria Adrammelech and his brother Sharezer killed their father while he was bowing downat the house of his god Nisroch at Nineveh. They then escaped to the land of Ararat, Esar-haddon, another son of Sennacherib.

Adramyttium.   A seaport city an Aegean sea, located in Mysia at the northwest corner of Asia Minor north of Pergamun. In modern Turky.

Adriel.   The son of Barzilla, from the city of Abel-meholah.

Adummim.   From root meaning red rocks. Ascent of Adummim. Is a steep pass about 12 km, 7.5 mi Ene of Jerusalem.

Agabus.   Agabus a Christian prophet who together with other prophets, come down from Jerusalem to Antioch of Syria during the year of Paul's stay there.

Agag.   The name of title applied to more than one king of the Amalekites. Ballaam, in his third prophetic utterance, foretold that king of Israel would be higher.

Agagite.   The belonging to Agag. A term applied to Haman and to his father, Hammedath, at Esther. 3:1, 10; 8; 3, 5; 9;24.

Agee.   A hararite the fathe of Shammah, who was one of David's mighty men - 2 Sa. 23:8, 11.

Agur.   The son of Jakeh & writer of the 30th chapter of the book of proverbs Pr. 30.1. He probably lived sometime during the period from Solomon reign 1037-998 B.C. to Hezekiah's reign 745-717 B.C.

Ahab.   Father's brother. Son of Omri & a king of northern kingdom of Israel. He ruled in Samaria 22 years from about 940 B.C. 1k. 16:28, 29.

Aharah.   The third son Benjamin. 1 Ch. 8:1 probably the as Ehi in Genesis 46:21 & Ahiram in Nubers 26:38.

Aharhel.   Descendant of Judah, a son of Harum 1. Ch. 4:8.

Ahasbai.   A Maacathite whose son Eliphelet was an outstanding fighter for David.

Ahasuerus.   The father of Darius the Mede mentiond at Daniel 9:1. The Ahasuerurs of Ezra 4:6. The Ahasuerus of book of Esther is believed to be Xerxes 1 son of the Persian king Darius the Great.

Ahav.   The nem given to a river or canal located in Babylonia.

Ahaz.   Shortened from of Jehoahaz, meaning may God take hold; God has taken hold. The son of king Jotam of Judah. Ahas began to reign at the age of 20 & continued for 16 years. 2Ki 16:2; 2 ch. 28:1.

Ahaziah.   God has taken hold. Son of Ahab and Jazebel & king of Israel for two years begining in about 919 B.C. He followed his idolttrous parents in Baal worship.

Ahban.   Son of Abishur & Abihali of the tribe of Judah 1. Ch 2:29.

Aher.   Another descendant of Benjamin. 1. Ch. 7:12.

Ahi.   From a root meaning brother. Son of Abdiel, a family head from the tribe of God 1 Ch. 5; 15.

Ahiam.   The son of Sharar the Hararite. One of Davids 30 mighty men of the military forces 1. Ch. 11:35.

Ahian.   Little brother. A son of Shemida. From tribe of Manasseh 1. Ch. 7:14, 19.

Ahiezer.   My brother is helper. Son of Ammishaddai & chieftain of the tribe of Dan.

Ahijah.   God is my brother. The fifth nemed son of Jerahmeel, of the tribe of Judah 1. Ch. 2:25.

Ahikam.   My brother has raised himself up. Son of Shaphan the royal secretary during Josiah reign.

Ahimaaz.   Father of Saul wife Ahinoam son of the priest Zadok and the father of Azariah 1. Ch. 6:8, 9, 53.

Ahimoth.	Possbly. Brother of death. A Lievite son of Elkanah. Of the family of Kohath. 1. Ch. 6:25.
Ahinadab.	Brother is willing.
Ahinoam.	Brother is pleasantness.
Ahio.	Shortened from of Ahijah; or possbly little brother. Son of Berieah & grandson of Elpaal, of tribe of Benjemin 1. Ch. 8:12-16.
Ahijah.	God is my brother. The fifth-named son of Jerameal, of the tribe of Judah. 1. Ch. 2:25.
Ahimoth.	Brother of death. A Lievite son of Elkanah of the family of Kohath. Ch. 6:25.
Ahinadab.	Brother is willing. One of the 12 deputies responsible to provid food for Solomon's royal household on monthly rotation.
Ahinoam.	Brother is pleasantness. King Saul's wife of Ahimaaz, and apparently the mother of Jonathan Isa 14:49, 50.
Ahio.	Shortened from of Ahijah; or probably, littel brother. Son of Beriah & grandson of Elpaal of trib of Benjamin 1 Ch. 8:12-16.
Ahira.	My brother is a companaion. The son of Enan and the chieftan of the tribe of Naphtali during the wilderness wandering.

Ahiram.   My brother is high. Son Benjamin & founder of a family.

Ahiramites.   Beloning to Ahiram family descended from Ahirama son of Benjamin.

Ahisamach.   My brother has supported Danite father of Oholiab, who the skilled with Bezale in constructing the tabernacle. Ex. 31:2-6; 35:34; 38:23.

Ahishahar.   Brother of the Dawan. Last nemed son of Bilhan and descended of Banjamin 1. Ch. 7:6, 10, 11.

Ahithophel.   A native of Giloh in the hills of Judah. Father of one of David's mighty men. Name Elian and probably the grandfather of Bath-Sheba.

Ahitub.   My brother is goodness. Descended of Aaron's son Ithamar, son of Phinehas and grandson of high prest of Eli.

Ahlai.   The daughter of Sheshan of the tribe of Judah.

Ahoah.   Ahohi. Ahohite a descendant of Benjamin through Bela 1. Ch. 8:1-4.

Aiah.   Black kite first named of two son of the Hivte Sheik Zibeon and uncle to one of Easu's wives Oholibamah Ge. 36:2.20, 24. 29; 1 Ch. 1:40 Father of soul concubine Rizpah.

Akan.   Last named of three son of Sheik Ezer of the Seirites. Ge. 36:20, 21, 27.

Akeldama. Field of blood the name applied by Jews to the plot of land the purchase of which resulted from the wages for unrighteosnes paid to Judas Iscariot for his betrayal of Christ Jesus. Ac. 1:18, 19. It has been identified as Hagged-Dumm. Meaning price of blood. On the S. side of vally of Hinnon on hill of Evil Canusel.

Akkub. Parbably. One seizing the heel; supplanter. Father of family of Nethinina who returned from Babylon with Zerubbabel. 537 B.C. Ezr. 2:12.45.

Alamoth. Maidens; young women evidently tearm musical execution.

ALLAMMECH. Al-lam'me-lech. Massive three of the kings a town in the territory alloted the tribe of Asher. Jos. 19:26.

Allon. Al-lon. Massive tree. Aimeonite descendant of Shemaiah 1. Ch. 4:37.

Almodad. First of Joktan's 13 son's; fourth generation after Shem; of Peleg.

Alphaeus. Al-phaeus. The father of Apostle Mattew <u>Levi</u>, the tax collector Mt. 9:9: Mr. 2:14. The father of James the less, the 9th listed of the 12 apasties Mt. 10; 3: Mr 3:18;.

Alvah. A Sheik of Edom and descendant of Esau Ge. 36.40, 43 1.Ch. 1:51 piabolly a place and tribe were also called Alvah.

Alvan. First-nemed son of Sheik Shobal Seirite Ge. 36; 20, 23, 29; 1 Ch. 1:40.

Amalek.   Am'a-lek. Amalekites. A mal.ek.tes. son of Esau's first born Eliphaz, by his son of Easu. Was one of the Sheik of Edom Ge. Son of Esau. Was one of the Sheiks of Adam, Ge. 36; 15, 16. Amalek's name also desiganated his tribal descendat's De 25; 17; Jg. 7:12; Isa. 15; 2.

Amanah.   Meaning trustworthy this name appears in Hebrew at Song of Solomon 4:8.

Amariah.   God has said. Priestly descendent of Aaron's son Eleazar through Phinehas; son of Meraioth; the father of Ahitub; grandfather of Zadok.

Amasa.   A.ma.sa. shortened from of Amasiah. Son of David sister of half sister Abigail and Jether Ithra. And cousin of Absalon and Joab. 2 Sa. 17:25. 1 Ch. 2:16, 17.

Amasai.   Shortend from of Amasiah. A Levite of family of Kohath; Son of Elanah and ancstor of prophet Samuel.

Amashsai.   Son of Azarel and one of the priests residing in Jerusalem in Nehemiahs time. Ne. 11:13.

Amaziah.   God is strong. A Levite of family of Meiari; son Hikiah.

Amittai.   Father of the prophet Jonah. From Gath-heler in Zebulun 2 Ki. 14:25; Jon. 1:1.

Ammiel.   People of God. Son of Gemalli of the tribe of Dan of 12 sent put by Moses to spy out the land of Canaan.

Ammihud. My peopl is dignity. An Ephraimite, father of Elishama, who was chieftan of tribe of Ephraim in the second year after coming out of Egypt 1512 B.C. Nu. 1.10; 2:18. He was an ancstor of Joshu. Jehosha. Jehoshua. 1 Ch. 7:26, 27.

Amminadab. My peopl are willing noble, generous. A son of Ram of the family of Hezron, thribe of Judah 1 Ch. 2:10 his son Nahshan.

Ammishaddai. People of the almighty. Father of Ahiezer, who as chiftain of tribe of Dan.

Ammizabad. My people have endwed. Son of Beneiah who was king David's mighty man over 30 outstanding fighter.

Ammon. The people. Lot's son by his younge daughter.

Amonon AmoNon. Thustworth; fater long lasting. David firstborn son by Ahinoam the Jezreelitess. Born at Hebron 2 Sa. 3 2. 1 Ch:3:1

Amorite. The Amorite appears among the list of son of Canaan.

Amos. Being aload carring a Lord. A prophet of God & writer of the book bearing his nam. Who lived in the ninth century B.C. Amons the propet.

Amptiatus From Lat. meaning enlarged. A beloved Christian brother in the congregetion at Rome, to whom the apostle Paul sent greeting Ro. 16:8.

Amaram.   People High Exalet - a grandson of Levi through Kohath. Ex. 6:16, 18, 20; Nu. 3:19; 26:58; 1 Ch. 6:18.

Amraphel.   King of Shinar southern Moesopotamia and an ally and supporter of King Chedorlamor of Elam.

Amzi.   Shortened from Amaziah meaning God is strong Levite of the family of Merari & an ancestor of Ethan.

Anah.   A son of Zibon & the father of Esau wife Oholibamah. Ge. 36: 2, 14, 18, 20, 24, 25. 1 Ch. 1:34, 40.4. Ohdibamah the daughter of Anah the daughter of Zibon.

Aank.   Probably, Long Necked. The name applied to a tribe of tall men. In Hebrew ha.Anag if it is the personal name of Arba the father of Anak Jos. 15.13 The name thereafter was also applied to his progeny compare Jos. 15.14 with. 14.15 where Arba is called the great man among the Anakim.

Anakim.   An'a-kim those of belonging to Anak. A race of people of extraodinary size who inhabited the mountain region of Canaan as well as some coastal areas.

Anamim.   Hamitic desendant of Mizraim since Mizraim becam synonymous with Egypt, it is probably that the Anamim settled there or in the area Ge. 10:13. Ch. 1:11. Cuneiform text of the time of Saigon 11 of Assyria.

Anammelech.   Posibly from Babylonin Anu is king. A deity of the Sepharvites that provid unable to deliver them from Assyrian aggresors 2 Ki. 18:34.

Anan.   Prably cloud. One of the head of the people of Israel whose representative.

Anani.   Probably a shortend from of Ananiah. A son of of Elioeai a postexillic descendant of king David. 1 Ch. 3:24.

Ananiah.   God has answered me. Father of Maasanah grandfather to Azariah, who assisted Nehemiah in rebulding the walls of Jerusalem. Ne. 3:23.

Ananias.   Hebrew name Hananiah, meaning God has show favor member of the early Christian congregation of Jerusalem. Following Pentecost of 33 C.E.

Anath.   A'nath. The father of one of Israel's judges, Shamgar Jg. 3:31; 5; 6. One of the three principal Canaanite goddesses. She is presented both as the sister & spous of Baal & as a symbol of lustful sex & war.

Anathoth.   A Benjamite. Son of Becher 1 Ch. 7:8.

Andrew.   Root meang man; male person; probably. Manly a brother of Simon Peter & son of Jonah Mt. 4:18; 16:17 while Andrew's native city was Bethaida, he & Simon were living together in Capernaum at the time Jesus called them to become fishers of men. Mr. 1:16. 17. 21. 29; Jah. 1:44.

Anub.   A descendat of Judah & son of Kos 1 Ch. 4:1, 8.

Apollonia.   Apollo place of Apollo a city of Macedonia named after the Greek sun-god Apollo.

Apllos.	Destroyer, abbreviation of Apollonius. A Jew of Alexandria, Egypt, posessed of notable elooquence in speaking & a sound knwledge of Hebrew scriptures.
Apostle.	The Greek word a.po.sto.los is deried from the common verb a-postel to meaning simply send forth or of Mt. 10:5. Mr 11:3.
Appaim.	From root meaing nose; nostril. Son of Nadab and descendat of Jerahmeel of tribe Judah. 1 Ch. 2:25 30.31.
Ara.	Son of Jether of tribe of Asher 1. Ch. 7:30, 38.
Arab.	A.Rab ambush. Town in the mountain of Judah mentiond along with Hebron, Duman, and other cities. Jos. 15:48, 52.
Arabah.	Ar.a.bah. Desert plain. That part of the extraordinary depression, or rift vally.
Arabia.	The Arabian pensula form part of the Asiatic continent.
Arad.	One of headman of tribe of Benjamine who at one time lived in Jerusalem 1 Ch. 8:15, 28.
Arah.	A.rah. Son of Ulla of the tribe of Asher. 1 Ch. 7:30.3 Head of a family whose member returned to Jerusllem from Babylon with Zerubbabel Ez. 2:1.2.5. Father or forefather of Shecaniah; the fater in law of Tobiah the Ammonite. Ne. 6:18.

Aram.	Son of Shem. Has five son's. Aram four son's: Uz. Hul. Gether and Mash. Aramaic is came from Aram. Now Syrians.
Ard.	One of seventy souls of the house of Jacob who came into Egypt Ge. 46:21.27. In the Genesis account he called a son of Benjamin.
Ardon.	One of the sons of Galeb the son of Hezron of tribe of Judah. Ch. 2:18.
Argob.	Glod of Earth.
Aridatha.	One of Haman's ten sons Es. 9.8.10.
Aieh.	Perhaps a man assanated in Samari in about 778. B.C. With King Pekahiah of Israel. By usurper Pekah 2. Ki. 15;25.
Ariel.	Altar heart of God; or lion of God. Moabite whose two son were kild by Beniah. 2 Sa. 23:20; 1 Ch. 11:22.
Arioch.	The king of Ellasar who in longue with Chedorlamor and two other kings. Shared in crushing the rebellion of Sodom. Gomorrah, and thir allies & in carrying of lot & his household. Abraham then overtook the victors defeated Arioch & his confederates.
Arkite.	Descendant of Ham through Canaan & one of the 70 post-flood family Ge. 10:17; 1 Ch. 1.15 the settled along the Mediteranean Coast W. of the Lebanon mountains.
Arnan.	Nam appearing in a list of King David's descendant Arnan lived after the return from Babylonian exil. 1 Ch. 3:1, 21.

Artaxerxes. Ar.ta.xerx'es a name or title applied in the Bible to two Persian kings.

Asahel. God has made. Son of David's sister or half sister Zeruiah and the brother of Abishai and Joab; hence. David nephew. Ch. 2:15, 16.

Asaiah. God has made. Descendant of Merari, live's third son, and a head of a paternal hous.

min-Asaph. God has gatherd. Son of live through Gershom. 1 Ch. 6.39.

Asarel. One of four son's of Jehallelel of tribe of Judah 1 Ch. 4:16.

Asenappar. This name appears in a portion of the book of Ezra. 4:10 recorded in Aramaic & is evidently a clipped rendering of the name of Assyrian King Ashurbanipal.

Asenath. The daughter of the Egyptian priest Potiphera of one giveng by pharoah to Joseph. As wife she becam the mother of Manaseh and Ephraim Ge 41:45, 50, 52. 46:20.

Ashbea. Let me make one sewear. Take an oath the hous of Ashbea descendant from Judah's son Shelah. Ch. 4:21.

Ashbel. Ashblites Ashbel was son of Benjamin, listed third at Genesis 46:21.

Ashdad. One of five principal cites of Phlistines with its worship of false god Dagon the other cities were Gath, Gaza, Ashkelan, & Ekron. Jos. 13:3 Ashdad.

Asher.	Meaning happy; happiness. The eighth son of Jacob and second of two sons through Zilpah, Leah maidservat Ge. 35:26. Asher's only full brother was Gad. Asher four sons & on daughter are listed at 1: Ch. 7:30.
Ashhur.	Ash hur possibly, blackness. Acording to Masoretic text, the son of Hezron born after his father's death; the great-grandson of Judah 1 Ch. 24:4-5, 24.
Ashima.	Ashima a deity worshiped by the people from Hamath. Whom the king of Assyria settled in Samaria after taking the Israelites into captivity. 2 Ki. 17:24.30 Ashima according to the Bablonian Talmud Sanhedrian 63b.
Astoreth.	Ashto-reth, a goddes of the Canaanites considered to be wife of Baal.
Asisel.	Made by God. Simeonite.
Asshurim.	Descendant of Dedan, son of Jokshon, one of Abraham's sons by Keturah. Ge. 25:1-3.
Assir.	Prisnoer - a Levite born in Egypt who was one of the sons of Korah - Ex. 6:24; 1 Ch. 6:22.
Atarah.	Grown one of wives of Jerahmeel of tribe of Judah and mother of Onam, Ch. 2:3-5, 25, 26.
Athaiah.	A man of tribe of Judah, a descendant of Perez.

Athlai.	Sons of Bebai; on of the Israelites who dismissed thir foregn wives after Esra came to Jerusalem in 468 B.C. Ez. 10:28.44.
Avvites.	Inhabitans of Avva. Who were among the people's whom the Assyrians used to replace exiled Israelites after capturing Samaria in 740. B.C. 2 Ki. 17:24.
Azaliah.	God has proved himself distinguished. Son of Meshullam & father of Shaphan the secretary of hous of God. 2 Ki. 22:3. 2 Ch. 34:8.
Azaz.	Shortend from Af Azaziah a descendant of Jacob first born son Reuben. 1 Ch. 5:1.8
Azazia.	Az.a.zi'ah God has proved superior in strength. One of six harpists in the procession that brought the ark of the covenant to Jerusalem.
Azel.	Azel distinguished man. A descendant of Saul through Jonathan' he had six son. 1 Ch. 8:33-38:9:43; 44.
Azgad.	Strong is Gad.
Azlza.	Strong one.
Azmaveth.	Death is strong. The father of Jeziel & Pelet of the tribe of Benjamin.
Azriel.	Azri-el God is my help. Father of prince Jerimoth, tribe of Naphtali in David's time 1 Ch. 27:19, 22.

Azrikam.   My help has risen up.

Azubah.   Left entirely; abandoned. One of the wives of Galeb the son of Hezron. 1 Ch. 2:18.19.

Azzan.   Meaning strong. Father of paltiel God chose to represent the tribe of Issachar at the division of the promised land Nu. 34:26.29.

Azzur.   One offering help. Father the false prophet Hananiah from Gibeon. Jer. 28:1.

Baal.   Ba al owner; Master. The fourth listed son of Jeiel. A Benjamine 1 Ch. 3:29.30:9:35.36.

Baaseiah.   A descendant of live through Gershom; ancester of temple musician. Asph 1 Ch. 6:39.40.43.

Babel.   Confusion.

Bak Buk.   Forefather of certian Nethinim. Who returnd to Jerusalm with Zerubbabel 537 B.C. Ezr. 2:4.51. Ne 7:53.

Baladan.   Bal a dan. Akkadian, meaning God has given a son. The father of Merodach-Baladan Isa. 39:1 Berodach. Balada at 2 Ki. 20:12. Baladan's son Merodach-Baladan was king of Babylon during at least part of the reign of king Hezekiah of Judah 745-717 B.C.

Bani.	Ba ni mirring Buildalevite in the line of Merari & ancestor of the Ethan whom David appointed.
Barkos.	Forefather of some Nethinim who returned to Jerusalem withe Zerubbel Ezr. 2:43.53; Ne. 7:46.55.
Bartholomew.	Bar.thol'o-mew. Son of Talmai.on of Jesus 12 apostes, generaily thouht to be Nathanael.
Baruch.	Bar.uch was the son of Neriah & brother Seraiah.
Becherites.	Becher an Ephramite family descendat from Becher. Nu. 26.35.
Bela.	The firstborn son of Benjamin & one of Jacob's household that came to Jacob into Egypt.
Ben.	Son. A Levite musician of David's day who accopied the Ark of the Covanaint to Jerusulem 1 Ch. 15:15.18.
Benaiah.	God has built son Levitical chief prist named Jehoiada & father of at least two sons Ammizabad & Jehoiada 1 Ch. 27:5.6.
Ben-Ammi.	Son of my people. Son of Lot by his younge daughter hence half brother of Moab Ben Ammi, also cold Ammon. Was forfather of Ammonites. Ge. 19:31-38.
Ben-Hadad.	Son of Hadad the nam of thre kings of Syira Hadad was the storm god worshiped.

Ben-Hanan. Son of the one showing favor; son of gracios one one of the four son of Shimen. Descendant of Judah. 1 Ch. 4:1, 20.

Benjamin. Son of Right Hand. Jacob's 12 son & full brother of Joseph. Benjamin appear to be the only son born to Jacb in the land of Canaan. Ch.

Beor. Be or. Edomite whose son Bela is listed as Edom's first king Ge. 36:31, 32 Ch. 1.43. Father of prophet Balam Nu.22.5

Beracah. Blessing.

Beved. Hail.

Bernice. Meaning conquer. Daughter of Herod.

Bethlehem. Hous of bread. A town in the Judean highland overlooking the principal higway leading to Jerusalem down to Beer-sheba. It is today cald Bitlahm.

Bichrites. Descendent of Benjamite Bichrior member of his family.

Bilgah. Brightening.

Bilcai. Brightening. A priest, or forefather of one who agreed to the covenant Nehemiah arranged Ne. 10:1.8.

Bishlam.   Bish-lam. In peace.

Bithiah.   Bi, thi, ah from Egyptian. meaning queen daughter of Pharaoh & his wife of
                Mered of tribe of Judah 1 Ch. 4:118.

Boaz.   Bo az in stenght. Boas son of Salma Salman & Rahab and was the father of
                Obed. Mt. t:5.

Bohan.   Proply thump descendant of Reuben after whom a boundray stone for terretory
                of Judah was named Jos. 15:6:18:17.

Bora-shan   Pit of smoke. One of places that David & his men frequented during his time
proply.   as fugtive. 1 Sa. 30:30,31.

Bukki.   Shortend from Bukkiah. Chieftain from the tribe of Dan.

Bukkiah.   From root meaning <u>flask</u>. Son Heman of the tribe Livi.

Bul.   From a root meaning <u>yield</u>; produce the eigh lunar month of the sacred
                calendar of the Israelites corresponding to the second month of the secular
                calendar 1 Ki. 6:37, 38. Ge. 7:11. It included part of October & part of November.
                Following the Babylonian exile. This month was calld Marheshvan.

Bunah.   Shortened from Benaiah meaing God has build. Son of Jerahmeel in the tribe
                of Judah; brother of Ram through whom the Messianic lineage is traced 1 Ch.
                2:3, 25.

Bunni.	Shortened from of Benaiah, meaning God has butt. A Levite whose descendant was chosen by lotto live in Jerusalem after the wall rebuilding by Ne.11.15.
Buz.	Abraham brother Nator by his wife Milcah; Rebekah uncle Ge. 22:20-23. His descendant were presumably Buzite, Eliha, Eliu's father being described as such Job. 32:2.6.
Bush.	Densely branched, shrub or cluster of shrub the Hebrew word Si'ach only four time at Ge. 2:5.21.15. Job. 30:4.7.
Caesar.	A Roman family name that became title in 46.B.C. Gaius Julius, Cassar was appointed dictator of Rome for ten years, but he was murdered in 44 B.C. Caesar was the name of his family Gaius being his personal name & Julius that of his clan or hous.
Caiaphas	Joseph. Caiaphas was the high pries during Jesus' Earthly ministry Lu.3:2. He was the son in low of high pries Annas Joh. 18:13. & was appointed to office by predecessor of Pontius Pilate, Valerius Gratus, about the year 18 CE.
Cain.	The first child born on Earth to Adam & Eve. <u>Something produce</u>.
Cainan.	Ca.i'.nan son of Enos Enosh; Cainan is evidently calld Kenan at Ge. 5:9-14 Chronicles 1:2.
Calah.	Ca lah a city founded by Nimrod in Assyria and part of the city of Nineveh, Calah, Resen and Rehoboth-Ir. The letter three places apparently being suburbs of Nineveh. Ge.10:9-12 Calah appears as Kalhu on Assyrian cuneiform texts & during the period of Assyrian empire, it became one of the three principal cities of the realm, along with Nineveh & Asshu, Calah was situated at the N E. angle of junction of the <u>Great Zab River</u> with Tigris.

Caleb.	Caleb. Ca.leb dog. Son of Hezron brother of Jerahmeel & great-grandson of Judah and Tamar 1 Ch 2:3-5.18; also called Chelubi 1 Ch. 2:9.
Candace.	Can.da.ce a queen of Ethiopia. <u>Habasha</u>. <u>Cush</u>. Whose treasures becam a Christian: Ac. 8:27.
Carmite.	Belonging to Carmi family descended from Garmi, a son of Reuben. Ne 26:5.6.
Casluhim.	Cas-lu'-him. A son or people descended from Mizraim the son of Ham.
Chaldean.	Chaldean originaly the land and people occupying the southeran portion of Babylonian aluvial plain the rich delta area of the Tigris & Ephrates rivers.
Chebar.	Che bar from <u>Babylonian</u>, meaning great <u>canal</u> a river in the land of the Chaldeans.
Chel-u-hi.	Descendent of Bani; one of those dismissing their foreign wives in the time of Ezra. 10 34.35.44.
Che sed.	One of the eight sons Milcah bore to Nahor, the brother of Abraham. Ge. 22:20-22.
Chidon.	The name of the owner of the threshing floor or the threshing floor itself where Uzzah was struck down be God. Whene an attempt was made to move the ark of the testimony in an improper manner from Kiriath-Jearim to City David.
Chileab.	Chil'e-ab David's second son born in Hebron his mother Abigail was the former wife of Nabal 2 Sa. 3:2.3 Chileab is called Daniel at Chronicle 3:1.

Chislev.	The name of the ninth Jewish lunar month which fell within November and December. Ne. 1:1. Je. 36:9 Zec. 7:1.
Chuza.	Herod Antipas man in charge possibly of the domestic affairs. Chuza's wife Joanna minsterd to Jeus. Lu. 8:3.
Cosam.	A descendat of Davids son Nathan; son of Elmadam & father of Additional; and ancestor of Jesus Mother Mary Lu 3:28.
Coz'bi.	Daughter of Zur, a Midianite chieftain. At the time 24,000 Israelites died for immorality in connection with Baal of Beor, Gozbi, along with the Simeonte Zimri who had brought her into his tent, was killed by having her genital parts pierced throuh by Phinehas. Nu 25:1,6-9.15.18.
Cush.	Ethiopia ??? in Arbic Habasha. Son of Ham. Son of Noah.
Cushi. Cushan.	Cush. Cushite. Ethiopian. Father of the prophet Zephaniah.1:1. Appear at Habakkuk 3:7 as paralleling the land of Midian or relates to a nighboring country. As shown on in the article Cush. Some decendant of Cush appear to have settled on the Arabian peninsula & the name Kusi or Kushim was anciently used to describe certain Arabic peoples of Regin.
Dagon	A god of Philstines.
Damascenes	Dam.a.scenes. Belong to Damascus the inhabitans of Damascus. 2 co 11.32 paul used the term when reounting his narrow escap from city. 20 year after Acts 9:23-25

Dan	Judge. The 5th of Jacobs 12 sons born in paddonaram Ge 35:25-26. Dan was the first born of his mother Bihak
Daniel	Dan-i-el May Judge is God. David's second son born to him at Hebron is Abigail ch 3:1 He is called chileab at 2 Samuel 3:3 with the slaying of first born Amoon.
Darkon	one whose descendant were represented among the Son of the servants of Solomon returning with Zerub babel ezr 2:1.2.5
David	possibly Beloved
Dedan	descendant of Abraham through Jokshon Ge.25:3. 1 ch 1:32. He settled part of Aribia
Delaiah	De La Lah God has Drawving up in Deliverance
Delilah	Dangling a woman living in the torrent Vally of Sorek. Delilah is introduced into Bible account toward the final part of Samson's 20 year Judgeship as the object of his love Jg.16:31
Dionysius.	God of Wien. An Areopagite of Judge of Athenian. Areopa
Dishon	possibly Antelope a Sante, sheik of Horite in the Land of Edim. Ge 36:20.21 1ch.1:38 Ge.36:28
Dodanim	Son of Javan

Dodo	ancestor possibly the grandfather of Judge tala of tribe o Ass
Drusilla.	The third & youngest daughter of Herod Agrippa I. About 38 C.E. Sester of Agrippa II, Bernice & Marlamne III her mother name was Cypros.
Dura.	The plain where Nebuchadnezzar set up a gold image Da. 3:1 The Akkadian term duru meaning circuit wall or walled place appears frequently in Mesopotamian place-name.
East.	Mizrach. Meaing sunrising ???
Ebed.	Servant father of gaal.
Eber.	From a root meaning pass over.
Eder.	A descendant of Beriah of the tribe of Benjamin who dwelt in Jerusalem. 1 Ch. 8:1, 15.16.28.
El.	God.
Ela.	Probably God, father of Shimei one of Solomon's 12 deputies who provided food for king & his houshold. 1 Ki. 4:7,18.
Elah.	Ela related to Hebrow El God. An Edomite Sheik who likely occupied the vilage of Eloth. Ge. 36.40.41.43. 1 Ch. 1:52.

Elasah.	God has made. The son of Shaphan who with Gemariah. Was sent by Zedekiah to Nebuchadnezzar in Babylon.
Elath.	E.lath possibly, Ram; or place of Ram Eloth Eloth plural.
Elead.	E'lead God has borne witnes.
Eleadah.	Ele-adah God has decked himself one of Ephraim's descendant's 1 Ch. 7:20.
gite Eleazar.	El-e-a zar God has helped. The third name son of High Priest Aaron by his wife Elisheba. Eleazar was of family of Kahath the son of Levi Ex. 6:16.18.20.23 Nu 3:2.
Elhanan. Achar Jg. 10.1	God has shawn favor; God has been gracious. Son of Jair who war with the Phlistines strakdown Lahmi the brother of Goliah the Gittite 1 Ch. 20:5 in 2 Samuel 21:19 Elhanan is indentified as son of Jaare-Oregime Bethlehamite.
Eli.	E.li ascended Gonllp high priest of Israel descandat of Aaron's fourt-named son Ithamar compare 2 Sa 8:17. 1 Ki. 2:27. 1 Ch. 24:3. Ex. 6:23. as high prist. Eli judge Israel for 40 years.
Eliab.	E.liab my God is father son of Helon of tribe Zebulun; one of the 12 chieftains.
Eliada.	E.li'a.da God has known. Son of David born Jerusalem 2 Sa. 5:13-16. 1 Ch. 3:5.8 called Beeliada at 1 Ch. 14:7
Ellam.	God of people. Father of Bath sheba. S 2a.11:3 called, Ammiel at 1 Ch. 3:5.

Eliasaph.	God has added incresed son of Deuel or Reuel of trib of gad.
Elidad.	My gad has loved. Son of Ghislon.
Eliel.	May God is God one of the head of half of the tribe of Manaseh.
Elienai.	Elie'nai shortend from Eliehe-enai. Descendant of Shimei of the tribe of Benjamin who dwelt in Jerusalem 1 Ch: 8:1.20.21.28.
Elijah.	My God is God. Prophet Elijah.
Eliphal.	Probably. My God has arbirated. The son of Ur listed among the mighty men of David military force.
Eliphaz.	Firstborn son of Esau. By his Cananite wife Adah six or seven of Eliphaz, son, including Teman, and Amalek, became Sheiks of Ed??? tribe Ge:36.4, 10-12, 15, 16. 1 Ch. 1:35-36.
Elishah.	Elishah E.li shah. Son of Javan a famliy from who the population of the isles of the nation was spread about Ge:10.4.
Elishaphat.	My God has judged.
Elishebat.	My God has judged.
Elishua.	God is salvation on of the sons born to King David in Jerusalem 2 Sa. 5:15, 1 Ch. 14:5. Eliphus is called Elishama at 1 Ch. 3:

Elizaphan.	My God has conceald. Son of Aaron's Uncle Uzziel who along with his brother Mislael at Moses direction carried the bodies of Nadab & Abihu outside the camp Ex. 6.22 Nu. 3:30.
Elizur.	My God is a rock. Son of Shedeur of tribe of Reuben: one of 12 chieftains who assisted Moses & Aaron in numbering the sons of Israel. Nu. 1:1-3, 5, 17:2:10.
El Maddm.	Ancestor of Jesus' earthly Mother Mary Lu. 3:28.
Elnaan.	God is pleasantness; God of pleasantness the father of Jeriboi. 1 Ch. 11:46.
Elnathan.	God has given. Father of King Jehoiachin's mother Nehushta 2 Ki. 24:8.
Elonites.	Elon. A family descendant from Zebulun's son Elon Nu 26:26.
Eluzai.	God is my strength.
Enosh.	Enos mortal man. Son of Seth, born to him at the age 105 years. Enosh was 90 years old where he becam father to Kenan & he lived a total 905 years Ge. 5:6-11.
Epher.	Son of Midian; grandson of Abraham by his wife Keturah Ge. 25:2.4 1 Ch. 1:33.
Ephram.	Son of Joseph by his wife Asenath, the daughter of Potiphera the priest of on. Ephraim the younger brother of Manasseh.

Esar-haddon.	From Assyrian, meaning Asshur gives a brother a younger son an succesor of Sennacherib, king of Assyrian.
Eshban.	The second-named son of Sheik Dishon; a descendant of Seir the Horite the Horite were the inhabiton of the land of Seir.
Eshton.	Son of Mehir. Descendant of Chelub of the tribe of Judah 1 Ch. 4:1.11.12
Ethiopia	Ethiopia was the name appiled by ancient Greek the region of Africa south of Egypt. <u>Hebrew name Gush</u>. Egyption text this region was likwise known by the name <u>Keesh Arabic name Habasha</u>, ancient <u>Greek name Ethiopia</u>.
Ethnan.	Hire gift a son of Ashur by his wife Helah. Ethnan was of tribe of Judah & family of Hezron. 1 Ch. 2:3.5.9.24;
Ethni.	Hire, gift descendant of live through his son Geshom the son of Zerah and of the musician Asaph. 1 Ch. 6:39-43.
Ezbai.	The father of Naarai, one the might men of King Davids military forces 1 Ch. 11:26; 37.
Ezbon.	Son of God & the grandson of Jacb. Ge. 46:16.
Ezekiel.	God strengthens. Son of Buzi a priest. He was among the captives taken to Babylon by Nebuchadnezzar along with Jehoiachim in 617 B.C. his first visios of God came to him in the thirtieh year in the fourth month.

Ezer.	Probably stor up one of the Horite Sheik in the land of Seir Ge. 361:20-21.
Ezra.	Help. An Aaronic prist. A descendant of Eleazar and Phinehas.
Ezrah.	Help. Name appearing in a list of Judahs descendant. Jether. Mered. Epher & Jalon are identfied as the sons of Ezra 1 Ch. 4:1.17.
Ezri.	My help. Son of Chelub and overseer of cultivator of the king's fields during David reign: 1 Ch. 27:26.
Gabriel.	Holy angel other than Michael named in Bible. Gabriel appeared to Daniel.
Gad.	Good fortune. Son of Jacob by Leah's maidservant Zilpah. Who also bore Gad's younger brother Asher.
Gaddi.	Gaddi probly good fortune. Son of Susi of the tribe of Manasseh.
Gaddiel.	Good fortune. Son of Sodi of the tribe of Zebulun.
Gadi.	From root meaning good fortue. Father of Israel's King Menahem. 2 Ki. 15:14.17.
Gaham.	Son of Abraham's brother Nahor by his concubin Reumah. Ge. 22:23, 24.

Gahar.	Nethinim family head. Som of whose descendant returned with Zerubabel from Babylonin exil in 537 B.C. Ezr. 2:1, 2, 43.47. Ne. 7:49.
Galal.	Ga.lal. Rolling: Rolled way. A Levite who returned from Babylonian. Exile. 1 Ch. 9:14, 15.
Gareb.	Gareb. One of David mighty men an Ithrite of the tribe of Judah. 2 Sa. 23:8.38. Ch. 2:4.5, 18.19.50.
Gatam.	Fourth named son Esau's firstborn Eliphaz. Gatam became one of the Sheik of the Son of Esau Ge. 36:10.11.15.16. 1 Ch. 1-36.
GAZEZ.	Ga.zez. Shearer first Chronicles 2:46 says Galeb's concubine Ephah give birth to Haran, Moza Moza & Gazez & than it satates that Haran became father to Gazez. Hence, there many have been two men named Gazez: 1-a son of Galeb and 2 - a grandson of Galeb.
GAZITES.	Ga'zites inhabitans of Gaza the word applying in bothe of its occurences to Phillistines Jos. 13:2.3 Jg. 16:1.2.
Genubath.	Son of Edomite prince Hadad.
Gera.	Alien resdent. Son of Benjamin's firstborn Bela. Ch. 8.1.3
Geshan.	The third named son of Jahdas of the tribe of Judah. Geshan is listed among the descendant of Galeb. 1 Ch. 2.

Geshem.	Ge'shem proply, downpour, pouring rain. An Arabian who along with Sanbaiah opposed Nahemiah in the rebulding of Jerusalem wall.
Geshur.	An Aramaean kingdom bordering on the Argo region of Bashan. East the Jordan River.
Gether.	Descendant of Aram son of Sham Ge. 10:22.23: 1 Ch. 1 17.
Geuel.	Geu el eminence of God son of Machi of the tribe of Gad.
Gibbar.	Gib'bar superior; mighty: overwhelming Gibba descendant returned with Zerubabel from Babylonia exile in 537 B.C. Ezr. 2:1.2.20.
Gibea.	Gib'e.a hill a descendant of Galeb of tribe Judah 1 Ch. 2:42.49.
Giddalti.	I have made great. Son of Heman. Levite singer who in David time.
Giddel.	Made great. An ancestor of a family of Nethinim temple slaves who were among those who returned with Zerubabel from Bablonian exil in 537 B.C. Ezr. 2:1.43.47. Ne. 7:49.
Gideon.	Gutter down. One who cuts off. Judges Israel. Son of Josh of family of Abi-Ezer of trib of Manasseh.

???

Gihon.	Gi.hon. Bursting fort: Gushing. One of four rivers that branched out of Eden, described as encircling the entire land of Cush. Ge. 2.10.13.
Gilead.	Gil.e.ad. Meaning witness heap Ge. 31:47.48. Son of Machir & grandson of Manasseh.
Ginath.	Father of Tibni the unsucessful rival of Omri for the kingship. Kingship over the ten tribe kingdom of Israel. 1 Ki. 21:22.
Gollath.	The giant from the city of Gath. of Philistine Army who was killed by David.
Gomer.	Gomer. Grandson of Noah & first named son of Japheth born after the flood. Ge. 10:1.2. 1 Ch. 1.4.5.
Haahashtari.	Ha.a.hash.ta.ri. A descendant of Judah. Son of Ashhur. 1 Ch. 4:1.5.6.
Habaiah.	Priest whose descendant returned from exile in Babylonia.
Habazziniah.	Descendant of Jonadab the son of Rechab. Jaazaniah the son of Jeremiah the son of Habazziniah. Was one of the Rechabites tested by by the prophet Jeremiah in the days of King Jehoiakim. Jer. 5:1-6.
Hacaliah.	Wait. Keep in expectation. Nehemiahs father Ne. 1:1:10:1.
Hadadezer.	Hadad is a helper. Son of Rehob & King of Zobah a Syrian Aramamean kingdom that is thought to have been situated north of Damascus. 2 Sa.8:3.5: 1 Ki. 11:23: 1 Ch. 18:3.5.

Hadar.	Successor to the kingship of Edom after the death of Baal-hanan: also called Hadad G. 36:31.39. 1 Ch. 1:43.50.51.
Hadashah.	New. Judean City in the Shephelah. Jos. 15:33.37
Hadlai.	Geasing. Father of the Amasa who was one of the heads of son of Ephraim in the days of King Pekah of Israel & King Ahaz of Judah 2 Ch. 28:6.12.16.
Hagabah.	Grasshopper an ancestor of family of Nethinim temple slaves the sons of Hagabah were among reteruring in 537. B.C. from exile in Bablon Ezk. 2:1.2.43
Hagar.	Sarh's Egyption maidservant's concubi & the mother of Ishmaeal.
Haggi.	Hag.gi. Born on a festival. The second named son of Gad; grandson of Jacob & ancestral head of the Haggites Ge. 46:8.16: Nu. 26:4.15.
Hagri.	Hagar father of Mibar: one of David might men 1 Ch. 11:26.38.
Hakkatan.	The small one father of Johanan of the family of Azgad accompanied by 110 males returned from Bablon with Ezra. 8:1:12.
Hakupha.	Head of family of Nethinim temple slaves. The son Hakupha are listed among these returning from Babylon in exile Ezr. 2:1.43.51. Ne. 7:6.46.53.
Halah.	A place to which Assyrian monarch transported Israelite captives 2 Ki. 17:6.18:11. 1 Ch. 5:26.

Ham.	One of Noah three sons born after 2470. B.C. Ge. 5:32 7:6:11:10. He was possibly the youngest son. Ge. 9:24.
Haman.	Son of Hammedatha the Agagite may mean that Haman was a royal Amalekite Es. 3:1. Haman was an Amalekite.
Hammath.	The father of the hous of Rechab & an ancestor of certain Kenites. 1 Ch. 2:55.
Hammedatha.	An Agagite: father of Haman
Hammoleecheth.	Ham.mo'le.cheth the queen. The sister of Manassah. Manasseh's grandson Gilead. She gave birth to Ishhod, Abi-ezer, and Mahlah. 1 Ch. 7:14.17.18.
Hammuel.	Ham.mu.el. Son of Mishma of the tribe of Simon 1 Ch. 4:24-26.
Hamor.	He-Ass. A Hivite chieftain: Father of Shechem. It was from the sons of Hamar that Jacob purchased a treat of land where he pitched his tent and than later set up an altar.
Hamutal.	Proply. Father-in law is Dew. Daughter of Jermiah from Libiah; wife of King of Josiah & mother of Jehoahaznah; and Mattaniah (Zedekiah). Both of whom reigned as kings over Judah 2 Ki. 23:30.31.24.17 Jer. 52:1.
Hanamel.	Son of Shallum the paternal uncle of prophet Jeremiah.

Hanani.	Propbly a shortened from of Hananiah. One of Heman's 14 sons. Hanani was designated by Lot to lead the 18 group of musicians at the sanctuary in the time of King David. 1 Ch. 25:4.6.9.25.
Hananiah.	Meaning God has shown favor. God has been gracious. Son of Shashak & head of a Benjamin house 1 Ch 8:1.24.25.28.
Haran.	Son of Terah & brother of Abraham & Nahar.
Hareph.	Meaning he has reproached. A descendant of Judah; son of Hur and father of Beth-gader. 1 Ch. 2:3.50.51.
Harhaiah.	Father of Uzziel. Harhaiah's son, a goldsmith.
Harhas.	Grandfather of Shalluna the husband of the prophetess Huldah. 2 Ki. 22:14.
Harhur.	Burning fever ancestral of family of Nethinim temple slaves. The son of Harhur are listed among those returning with Zerubbabel from Babylonin 537 B.C. Ezra. 2:1.2.43.51: Ne. 7:46.53.
Hariphite.	Belong to Harph.
Haroeh.	The seer one listed in the genealogy of Judah as a son of Shobal. 1 Ch. 2:3.
Harum.	A man of the tribe of Judah 1 Ch. 4:1:8.

Hashabiah.   God has accounted considered. Al Levite in the line of descent from Merari to the temple Le Singer Ethan, 1 Ch. 6:3.

Hashem.   The sons of Hashem the Gizonite are listed among David's mighty men 1 Ch. 11:26.34.

Hasupho.   The forfather of a family of Nethinim. Member of which returned from Bablon with Zerubbel in 537 B.C.

Hathath.   Son of Othniel. The son Kenaz. Probably by Galeb daughter Achsah; 1 Ch 4:13, Jos. 15.17.

Hatita.   Ha.ti.ta ancestor of family of temple gatekeeper which returned from Bablon 537 B.C.

Hattil.   Hat.til. A paternal head of son's of the servant of Solomon who returned to Jerusalem from Babylon with ???

Hattush.   A head priest who returned from Babylon with Zerubbel in 537 B.C. Ne. 12:1.2.7.

Hazael.   God beheld antable king of Syria.

Hazarmaveth.   Courtyard settlement o death. A descendant of Noah through Shem and Joktan. Ge. 10:1, 21.25.26. 1 Ch. 1:20.

Hazo.	Probably a shortened from of Hazael. Meaning God Beheld. Beheld a nephew of Abraham. Fifth named son of Nahor & Milcah. Ge. 22:20-22.
Heber.	Partner. Son of Beriah and grandson of Asher; ancestral head of the Heberites. Ge. 46.17; Nu. 26:45. 1 Ch. 7:30-32.
Hebron.	Grandson of Levi & son of Kohath. Forefather father of son's of Hebron or Hebronites. Ex. 6:16.18. Ne. 3:19.27. 26:58, 1 Ch. 6:2. 18:15:4.9.23.12.19. 26:30:32.
Hebronites.	Belong to Hebron a Levite family descendant from Kohaths son Hebron. Ex. 6:16.18. Nu. 3:27.26.58: 1 Ch. 26.23.24.
Heldai.	Probably mole rat. Descendant of Othniel. 1 Ch. 27:1.15.44.47.
Heleb.	Son of Baanah the Netophathite.
Helek.	Shortend from of Hilkiah meaning my portion. Share.
Helem.	Descendant of Asher whose family is listed in genealogy of the tribe. 1 Ch. 7:36.40.
Heman.	Desirable one of the sons of Dishon. Who was a son of Seir the Horite Ge. 36:20.21.
Helez.	He has recued one of David mighty man Paltite or Peloninte 25a 23.26. 1 Ch. 11:26.27.

Heli.   Hebrew meaning high exalted father of Mary & mater.

Helaki.   Short from of Hilkiah meaning my portion share.

Helkath.   Smooth pleace sites of tribe of Asher Jos. 19:24:25.31.

Heman.   Son of Loton & descendant of Seir the Horite. Ge. 36:20.22.

Hemdan.   Desirable one of the son of Dishon who was son of Seir the Horite Ge. 36.20.21.26.

Hepher.   He has searched out son of Gilead & great-grandson of Mansseh; ancestor of Hepherites Nu. 26.29.

Hephzibah.   My delight is in. Wife of Hezekih & mother of King Mansseh 2 Ki 20: 21: 21:1.

Heres.   Sun.

Hermes.   One of Christians in congregation at Rome to whom Paul sent personal greeting Ro. 16:14.

Herodias.   The wife of Herod Antipas who through her daughter Salam. Regsted & reieved the head of Johan Baptizer in 32 C.E. M??? 6:22-28.

Hesed.   Short of Hasadiah loving-kindness.

Heth.   The second-listed son of Canaan & great-grandson of Noah through Ham. Ge.
                  10:1.6.15. 1 Ch. 1.13 Heth was ancestral fathe of the Hittites. 1 Ki. 10:29. 2 Ki. 7:6.

Hezekih.   God sterenghtens king of Judah 745-717 B.C He apparently became king when
                  his father Ahaz died, in the third year of Hoshea, king of Israel.

Hezion.   Grandfather of the first King Ben-hadad of Syria.

Hiel.   Hi.el. Short of ahiel mean my brother is God. A Bethelite who rebuilt Jericho
                  during Ahab reign in tenth century B.C.

Hiram.   Hi ram. Probably short of ahiram my brother is high.

Hiram.   Hi ram - abi. My father.

Hiram-ABiv.   Hiram his father

Hittites.   Belong to Heth a people descendant from Heth name son of Canaan Ge. 10.6.

Hivites.   A people descended from Canaan the son of Ham Ge. 10:6.15.17 Ch. 1:13,15
                  Hivite inhabited the city of Sheehem in the days of the pariarch Jacob.

Hophni.	From Egypt mean tadpole one High Priest Eli sons, Hophni & his brother Phinehas were good for nothing man.
Hophra.	Egyp mean is the heart of Ra, the Son God endures.
Horam.	King of Gezer one of the 31 kings defeated by Isralites under the leadership of Joshua during the conquest of the promised land.
Hori.	Descendant of Seir the Horite through Lotan Ge. 36:20-22. 1 Ch. 1.39. Simeonite whose son Shaphat was on of the 12 spies sent out by Moses from the wilderness of Paran Nu. 13:2.3.5.
Horite.	A people inhabiting the mountains of Seir in patriarchal time.
Hormah.	Hor.mah. Devoting to destruction. City in southern part of territory of Judah 1 Ch. 4:3:30.
HOSEA.	Ho'sea sorten from of Hoshiah Hebrew prophet and writer of the Bible book of Hosea.
Hoshama.	Sorten from name Jehoshama mean God has heard.
HOSHEA.	Shorten from of Hoshaiah. On of the 12 sent by Moses to spy out the land of promise in 1512 B.C. Son of Nun of the tribe of Ephraim.
Hul.	Son of Aram Ge. 10:23.

Hupham.	Huphamites belong to Hupham also called Hupham was son probably a leater descendant of Banjamin & ancestral head of Huphamite Ge. 46:8, 21 Nu. 26.39.
Huppim.	Son or descendant of Benjamin included in the list of those who came into Egypt with Jacobs household in 1728 B.C.
Huri.	Gadit descendant through Buz. 1 Ch. 5:11, 14.
Hushah.	Son or city fathered or founded by Ezer of the tribe of Judah. 1 Ch. 4.1.4.
Ibri.	Son of Jaaziah a Merite Levite of King Davids time. 1 Ch. 24.27.30.31.
Iddo.	Shortened from of Adaiah mean God has decked. Son of Joah a Levite of family of Gersham 1 Ch. 6:19-21.
Iezer.	Sorten from of either Ab Zezar or Ahiezer. Iezcrites shortened from of the Abi-ezer.
IGAL.	May God redeem.
Igdaliah.	Geot is God. Father of Hanan Jer. 35.3.4.
Imlah.	May God fill or may God cause father of Micaiah. A prophet of God contemporaneous with King Ahab & Jehoshaphat 1 Ki. 22:8.9. 2 Ch. 18.7.8.
IMNITES.	Belong to Imanh. Family of the tribe of Asher descendent from Imnah Nu. 24:44.

IMNA.   Im.na. God has hold back with held. Son of Helem valiant, mighty man and head of a paternal house of the tribe of Asher 1 Ch. 7:35.40.

IMNAH.   May God appointed or numberd. First name son of Asher & forefather of the Imnites Ge. 46:17. Nu. 26:44. 1 Ch. 7:30.

Im.rah.   He rebels. Son of Zophah: a paternal head of chieftains of the tribe of Asher a valiant mighty man 1 Ch. 7:36.40.

IMri.   Im.ri sortened from of Amariah mean God has Sasid. Son of Bani the tribe of Judah through Perez 1 Ch. 9:4.

INUIA.   Area designated by the Bible name India is uncertain Es. 8:9. The area drined by the Indus River & its tributaries that is Penjab reginn also sind. Likely the Indus valy was setteld not long after the language of Babeles, bulders was confused a comparison of ancient civilization of the Indus valy with that Mesopotamia reveals the erectoin of structures like the Ziggurt platform of Mesopotamian sculpture, and pictographic singns that bear a resemblance to early Mesopotamian form. Assyrialogist Samuel N Kamer has sugest that Indus valy was settled by a people who fled from Moesopotamia when the Sumerian took control of the area.

Iph-deiah.   May God redeem son of Shashak a head man of the tribe of Benjamin. Ch. 81.25.28.

Iphtah-El.   I.ph-tah-el. God has opened. A valley on boundary between the tribes of Zebulun & Asher Jos. 19.10.2.

Ir.   Full grown ass. Father of Shuppin and Huppim 1 Ch. 7:12. Probably the same as the Benjamin Iri. Ch. 7:7.

Ira.	I.ra.ful grown ass. Jairite listed among King David's leading officer as priest of David. 20:26. Ira propably was a descendant of the Jair mentionted at Numbers 32:41.
Irad.	Grandson of Cain, forefathe of the bigamist Lamemch and of Jabal and Tubal Cain. Ge. 4:17:23.
Iram.	Probably from root mean full grown. Sheik or chieftain of Esau.
IRI.	I'ri. Propably from root mean full grow ass. Son of Bela. 1 Ch. 7:7. Iri. Propably the Sam as Ir of 1 Chronicle. 7:12.
IRIJAH.	God sees son of Shelemiah the son of Hananiah. The officer in charge of the gate of Banjamin in Jerusalem who arrested Jeremiah on the fals charge of intending to desert to the Babylonian Jer 37:13.14.
Irpel.	Ir'pe.el. May God healed. City of Benjamin Jos 18:21.27.
Ir Shemesh.	City of Sun. Town boundary of Dan.
Iru.	Propbably from root meaning full grown.
Isaac.	Laughter. Son of Abraham from his wife Sarah.
Iscah.	Iscah. Daughter of Abraham's brother Haran, and sister of Lot. She was born before her Uncle Abraham. And houshold left Ur of the Chaldees. Ge. 11:27.31.

ISCARIOT.   Is.car.i.ot. Probably. Man from Kerioth. Or apastel Judah & his father Simon. Mt. 10:4. Lu. 6:16.

Ishbah.   My he still calm descendant of Judah; father of Eshtemoa. 1 Ch. 4:4.7.

Ishbak.   Ish'bak. The fifth lisled of six son's taht Keturah bore to Abraham which son's Abraham sent a way with gifts but withhout a share of his inheritance Ge. 25:1.2.5.8. 1 Ch. 1:32.

Ishbi.   Benob one of four sons of Rephaim the giant race of Canaanites who were prominent during the last wars with Israel in David's reign. Ishi-Benob. Carried a copper spear weighing 300 shekels 34 kg: 7.5 lb.

Ish-Bosheth.   Mean a man of shame youngest of Sauls four son's and his suceesor to the throne. Ish-Basheth-anam in which Baal is replaced by Boshet 2 Sa. 2:10.

Ishhod.   Is-hod. Man of dignity. A descendant of Manasseh whose mother was Hammolecheth. 1 Ch. 7:14.18.

Ishi   Ish'i. Short from of Isaiah, mean Salvation of God. Descendant of Judah son of Appaim and father of Sheshan 1 Ch. 2:3.31.

???

Ishmael.   Sort from of ISMAEL an en early descendant of Judah 1 Ch. 4:1.3.

Ishmael. Ish'ma-el. God hears. Listens. Son of Abraham by Sarah's Egyptian. Slave girl Hagar born in 1932 B.C. His father Abraham being 86 years old at the time. Ge. 16:14-16.

Ish.ma'iah. May God hear. Listen on outstanding <u>Gibeonite</u> warrior who joined Davids Army a Ziklag before bef soul's death. 1 C. 12.1.4.

Ishmerai. May God guard ahead among the Benjamin who lived in Jerusalem. Son or descendant of Elpaal. 1 Ch. 8:1.18.28.

Ishpan. Mean sweep bare ahead of people among the Benjamin living in Jeursalem. Son or descendant of Beriah 1 Ch. 8:1, 16.28.

Ish.tob. Man of tab. One of the smal kingdoms that provided fighting men for the sons of Amman to use against David.

Ishvah. Ish'vah. Mean probably. Made Equel. Smooth out the second of Ashere the four son's Ge 46:17 Ch. 7:30.

Ishvites. Ishvi a family descendant from Ishvi son of Asher.

Israel. Contened persiverer with God; or God contends.

ITHAI. Probably a short from of Ithiel. Son of Ribal from Gibeah in Banjamins territory. One of mighty men of David's military forces 1 Ch. 11:26.31.

Ithamar. Propably father or brother of palm tree the fourth lested of Aarons sons ex. 6.23. Nu. 26:60.

Ithiel. Propably. With me is God propably son on discple of Agur. Pr. 30:1.

Ithlah. Propably mean hang. One of border cities of Dan Jos. 19.40.42.

Ithra. Mean more than enoug; overflow. Father of Amos by Davids sister of half sister Abigail 2 Sa. 17.25.

Ithran. Mean more than enough. Overflow son of the Edomite Sheik Dishon. Descendant of Seir the Horite Ge. 36.20.

Ithrem. From root mean more than overflow David six sons born in Hebron by his wife Eglah. 2 Sa. 3:5, 1 Ch. 3.1.3.

Ithrite. Belong to Jether or Jethro family name in tribe of Judah connected with Kiriot-Jearim. 1 Ch. 2:3.52.53.

Ittai. Shortened from Ithiel. Propably with me is God.

Jaareshiah. Family head in the tribe of Banjamin. Son or descendant of Jereham. 1 Ch. 8:1.27.28.

Jaasiel.   May God make; God has made.

Jaazaniah.   God has given ear.

Jaaziah.   Meiavite Levite four of whose sons or descendant served during Davids reing.
                1 Ch. 24:26.27-31.

Jaaziel.   Levite musician in the second division that accompanied the ark of the coveant
                when transfered from Obededoms hous to Jerusalme 1 Ch. 15:18.

Jabal.   Ja.bl. descendant of Cain; son; of Lamech & his first wife Adah. Ge. 4:17.19.20.

Jabez.   Mean pain descendant of Judah named Zabez by his mother because of her
                pain in givin birth to him.

Jabin.   Ja.bin propably discirnin; understanding or one who builds perhaps dynastic
                nam or title of the Canaanite King of Hazo. King of Hazor whene Joshua
                invaded the ???

Jab'neel.   Jab'ne'el. May God bulid.

Jabneh.   May God build.

Jacan.   Related through a play on word to the Acher. Mean ostaracism. Fifth named
                of Abihails seven sons a Cadite 1 Ch. 5:15:13.14.

Jachin.	May God firmly establish the fourth listed son Simeom Ge. 46:10.
Jachinites.	Belong to Jachin descendant of Simon. Jachin Ge. 46:10. Nu. 26:12.
Jackol.	Kind wild dog & closely to the fox.
JACOB.	One seizing the heel. Supplnter. Son of Isac & Rebekah and younger twin brother of Esau.
Jaddua.	Mean know.
Jahdo.	Propably may he feel glad one me in genealogy of God tribe. Son of Buz and father of Jeshishai 1 Ch. 5:11.14.
Jahleeltes.	Descendant of Jahleel of tribe of Zebulun. Nu. 26:26.
Jahzeiah.	May God behold.
Jahzerah.	Priest whose descendant lived in Jerusalem after the Babylonian exile 1 Ch. 9:12. He is propably the same as Ahzai in Nehemiah 11:13.
Jair.	Ja ir. Descendant of Judah throgh his grandson Hezron. Hezron married a woman from the tribe of Manasseh 1 Ch. 2:21.22.

Jairit.	Belonging to Jair the designation of Ira the priest of David. 2 Sa. 20.26.
Jakeh.	Father of Agur. The writer of what is record in proverbs 30-Pr. 30-1.
Jakim.	Short from of Jakimiah. Mean God has raised up descendant of Banjamin through Shimei included in a listed of head of father's houses residing in Jerusalem 1 Ch. 8:1. 19-21.28.
Jalon.	Deseandant of Judah. One of the sons of Ezrah 1 Ch. 4:17.
Jalam.	Ja lm. Son of Esau by his wife Oholibamah. Jalam was born in Canaan but was soon taken to Edom Seir where he eventualy became a Sheik. Ge. 36.5.6.8.14.18. 1 Ch. 1:35.
Jambres.	A resister of Moses one of the Egyption in the Court of Pharaoh. 2T 3:8. Ex. 7:11.
James	English equivalent of Jacob. Mean one seizing the heel; supplanter. Fathe Apostl Judah not Judas Iscariot. Lu. 6:16, Ac. 1:13.
Jamin.	Right hand. The second listed son of Simeon Ge. 46:10. Ex. 6:15. Ch. 4:24. He founded the family of the Jaminites. Nu. 26:12.
Jaminites.	Belong to Jamin descendant of Jamin of Simeon's tribe Nu. 26:12.

Jamlech.	May God case to reign. One of chieftains of the tribe of Simeon who in the day of King Hezekiah extended their territory into the valley of Gedor 1 Ch. 4:24.34.38.41.
Janai.	Propably may God has answerd. Gadite residing in the territory of Bashan. 1 Ch. 5:11, 12
Jannai.	Jan nai ancestor of Jesus mothe Mary; the fifth generation prior to her. Luka 3:24.
Jannai	Jan nai. Aresister of Moses with whom Paul compares apostutes who resist the truth 2 Ti. 3:8.9.
Janoah	Ja.no.ah. From root that means yest, settle down. City in the ten tribe kingdom take b Tiglath-Pileser III during Pekah's reign C778-759. B.C. Its inhabitan's were deported to Assyria 2 Ki. 15:29.
Japheth.	Ja.pheth. May he grant ample space. Son of Noah. Brother of Sham & of Ham. Japheth the eldest of the three sons Ge. 10:21. Japheth the oldest.
Japhia	Ja.phi.a. May God beam forth. The king of Lachish who joined forces with four other Amorit kings to punish Gibeon for making peace with Israel. Jas. Gibeons. Son of David born at Jeursalme. 2 Sa. 5:14.15. Ch. 3:7; 14:6.
Japhlet.	May He provid escape. A descendant of Asher.

Japhletites.   Belong to Japlet an ancient people occupying territory on Ephraim's boundary when the Israelites moved into the promised land. Jos. 16.3.

Jarah.   Descendant of Saul through Jonathan & according to this genealogy. Himself a father of three son's. Ch. 9:39. He called Jehoaddah at Chronicles. 8:36.

Jared.   Father of Enoch.

Jarha.   Egyptian slave of Judah's descendant Sheshan since Sheshan had no sons he gave his daughter in marrige to Jarha.

Jarib.   May God contend. God has conducted our legal case.

Jarmuth.   From root mean. Be high exalted. One of five Amarite cities.

Jason.   Propable from root mean. Heal. Promiment Christian in Thessalonica.

Jaroah.   Descendant of God who resided in the territory of Bashan 1 Ch. 5:11.14.

Jashen   Propably. Sleeping; falling a sleeping. The sons of Jashan is found in the list of David mighty men 2 Sa. 23:32.

Jashobeam.   Propably the people haved returned. Korahite warrior who joined David forecs at Ziklag 1 Ch. 12:1-6.

Jashub	Propably. He has returned the third listed son of Issachar and founder of the Jashubite division of his tribe. 1 Ch. 7:1. Nu. 26.23.24. He is called Job at Genesis 46:13.
Javan.	The fourth son of Japheth.
Jazer.	May God help an Ambrite city with dependent towns located east of Jordan in the time of Moses the Israelites.
???	Took dazer & the surronding region Nu. 21:25.32.
Jebus ???	Propably mean tread down. Jebusite. Jebus was an ancient city of Jebusites on the site now Jerusalem.
Jedidah.	Beloved. Wife of Amon & mother of King Josiah whom she bore in 667 B.C. daughter of Adaiah from Bozkth. 2 Ki. 21:24-26:22.1
Jehezkel.	Je.hez.kel. May God strengthen; the priest & head of the paternal hous that was selected by Lot for the 20th of 24 roting group into which David had the priestly services divided. Ch. 24.1.3.7.16.
Jehiel.	May he live, O God.
Jehieli.	Jehiel a Gershonite Levit who apparently served as on overseer of sanctuary's treasury Ch. 26:20-22.

Jehoaddin.   God is pleasure mother of Judah's King Ahmazial wife of Jehoash 2 Ki. 11:1.2.

Jehoahaz.   May God take hold.

Jehoash.   King of Judah for 40 years from 898 to 859 B.C. he was the youngest son of Judah son of Judahs King Ahaziah.

Jehohanan.   God has shown favor or cracious.

Jehoiarb.   May God contend. First of the 24 prestly divison organaizd during Davids rule 1 Ch. 24:1-3.5-7.

Jehondab.   God is willing. Jonadab short from Jehonadab.

Jehonatan.   God has given.

Jehoram.   God is exalted short from of the name is Joram.

Jehoshabeth.   God is plenty daughter of King Jehoram & wife of High Priest Jehoiada.

Johosheba.   God is plenty. Wife of High Priest Jehoiada; daughter of King Jehoram of Judah.

Jehoshua.   God is salvation son of Nun; an Ephramaite who succeded Moses & led Israelites into the promised land.

Jehozabad.	Jehoza.bad. Propably God has endowed the second of Obed-edoms eight sons included among the sanctury gatekeeper 1 Ch. 26:1.4.5.13.15.
Johozadak.	Je.haz.a.dak. Propably God pronounce righteous Jozadak. Jo.zaa.dak short from Johozadak uesd in Nehemiah, longer from elsewhere.
Jehubbah.	Je.hub.bch leading member of the tribes of Asher 1 Ch. 7.3.40
Jeiel.	Je.iel a descendant of Jacab's son Reuben. Enseñanza 5:1-7.
Jekabzeel.	God has collected. An alternat from the name Kabzeel Ne. 11:25.
Jekameam.	Jek.a.me.am. May people rise up the fourth son of Hebron. A Kohathite Levite, & founder of Levitcal paternal hous that survived at least until David reign 1 Ch. 23:12.19.24-23.30.
Jekamiah.	God has raised up. Descendat of Judah & son of Shallum. 1 C Ch. 2.3.41.
Jekuthiel.	A descendant of Judah and father of Zanoah. 1 Ch. 4:1, 18.
Jemima.	Je.mi.mah the first son of Jobs three daughters born after his great test Jemima & sisters most beautifl women in all land. Job. 42:13-15.
Jemuel.	Jem.u.el. Propaly. Day of God. The first named son of Simeon & one of the seventy numberd among Jacobs houshold came into Egypt. Ge. 46:10.27. Ex. 6.15.

Jephthah.	Jeph.thah. May God has open. A judg of Israel of the tribe of Manasseh Nu. 26:29. Jg. 11.1.
Jerahmeel.	Je.rah.me.el May God show mercy firstborn of Judah's grandson Hezron.
Jered.	Je.red a descendant of Judah & father of those who setteld Gedor. 1 Ch. 4:1.18.
Jeremai.	Jer.e.mai. Short from of Jeremoth or Jeremiah. One of the seven sons of desandant of Hashum who had taken foreign wives but sent them away. Ezr. 10:25.33.44.
Jeremiah.	Porpably God loosens from the womb. Benjamite who joined David when he was at Ziklag he was among David mithey men 1 Ch. 12:1.4.
Jermoth.	Mean be high. Descendant of Banjamin throgh his son Becher Ch. 7:6.8.
Jeribai.	Jeri.bi. May contend he has conducted our legal case. One of David mighty men; son of Elnaan. 1 Ch. 11:26-46.
Jericho.	Jer.i.cho propably Moon City the first Canaanite city west of the Jordan to be conquered by Israelites Nu. 22:1. Jos. 6:1.24.25.
Jeriel.	Jeri el May God see. Son of Tola & head of paternal hous in the tribe of Issachar 1 Ch. 7:1.2.
Jerimoth.	Mean be high. Exalted son or descendant of Banjamin's firist born Bela & valiant mightymen. 1 Ch. 7:6-7.

Jeroboam.	Two kings of Israel whose reigns were separated by some 130 years. First king of the ten tribe kinkdom of Israel; the son of Nebt, one of Solomons offcers in the village of Zeredah; of tribe of Ephraim.
Jerubbesheth.	Je.rub.be.sheth. Let the shameful thing make a legal defense. The name of Judge Gidean found at 2 Samuel 11:21. Evidently this is form of Jerubbaal, the nam given to Gideon by his father Doash when Gideon pulled down the altar of Baal Jg 6:3-32.
Jeruel.	Propably laid erected by God.
Jerusalem.	The name of Jersalem land of peace. The earliest recorded name of city is Salem Ge. 14:18.
???	
Jerusha.h.	Je.ru'sha h he has taken possession. Mother of King Jotham; wife of Uzziah; daughter of Zadk 2 Ki. 15:32.33. 2 Ch. 27 1.2.
Jeshaiah.	God is salvation. Levitical descendant of Moses through Eliezer & an ancestor of Shelamoth whom David appointe as on of his treasurers 1 Ch. 23:15; 26.24:28.
Jesharelah.	Jesh.a.re.lah. Son of Asaph listed among the musicians & singers in Davids time. 1 Ch. 25:1.9.14. He is propably the same as Asharelah. 1 Ch. 25.2.
Jeshebeab.	May father continue to dewel or passibly. God has broght the father back.

Je'sher.   Uprightness. Son of Cajeb the son of Hezron; of tribe of Judah 1 Ch. 2:3.5.18.

Jeshimon.   Desert, abave wilderness area seemingly at N.E. end of Dead Sea Beth-
                Jeshimoth was perhaps located.

Jes'hishai.   Je'shishai. Mean aged descendant of God 1 Ch. 5:11.15.

Jeshohaiah.   Jesh.o.hai ah. Semeonite chieftain. One of those who expanded their
                territory at the epense of Hamites during the days of King Hezekiah 1 Ch.
                4; 24.34-41.

Jeshua.   Jesh.ua. Propably short from Jehoshina mean God is salvation.

Jesh'urun.   Upright one.

Je.simi-el.   May God set appoint. One of Simeon't chieftain who in King Hezekiah's day.
                Extended their territory to east of valy of Gedor. 1 Ch. 4.24, 34-41.

Jesus.   In Heb Ye-shu'a. In Arabic Yesoa ???.

Jether.   Mean mor than enough; overflow. Moses father in law Jethero is called Jethro
                in the Masoretic taxt Exodus. 4:18.

Jetheth.   Je.theth Sheik of Edom. Descendant of Esau. Ge 36.40.43 1 Ch. 1:51.

Jethro.	Jethro mean more than enough. Moses father in law a Kenite Ex 3:1. Jg. 1:16.
Jetur.	Je tur. Son of Ishmael Ge. 25:13.15. 1 Ch. 1:31.
Jeuel.	Levite who helped in cleansing the templ during Hezekiah reign a descendant of Elizaphn. 2 Ch. 29:13.15.16.
Jeush.	Je ush. Propably, may he lend aid son of Esau by his Hivite wife Oholibamah.
Jeuz.	Je uz. He has conseled. Advised family head in the tribe of Benjamin; son of Shaharaim by his wife Hodesh.
Jew.	Belong to Judah - person pelong to tribe Judah.
Jezer.	He has formed the third son of Naphtali founder of the family of Jezerites. Ge. 46:24. Nu. 26:48.49. 1 Ch. 7:13.
Jezerites.	Belong to Jezer Nu 26.48.49.
Jeziek.	A Benjamin son of Azmaveth. 1 Ch. 12:1-3.
Jezreel.	God will sow seed - descendant of Judah. Propably the forefather of the inhabitans of Jezreel. 1 Ch. 4:1.3.

Jidlaph.	The seven of the eight sons borne to Nahor by his wife Mileah. Jaidlph was therfore a nephew of Abraham & an uncle to Isac's wife Rebekah, Ge. 22:20.23.
Joann.	Short feminine from of Jehohanan mean God has shown favor.
Jo'ash.	This name is spelled two ways in Hebrew, though only as Joash in English - the first & more common, Yoh'ash, is a short from of Jehoash.
Job.	Man living in the land of Uz in what is now Arabia. Job. 1:1. Uz son Aram. There is no one like him in the earth. A man blameless and upright fearing God & turning asid from bad Job. 1:8.
Jobab.	Descendant of Sham throgh Jaktan Ge. 10:21.25.29. 1 Ch. 1:23 exact region settled by offspring is not known today. Son of Zerah from Bozrah; an Adomite.
Jochebed.	Propably God is glory. A daughter of Levi who married Amram of the same tribe & became the mother of Miriam Aaron & Moses. Ex. 6:20. Nu. 26.59.
Joda.	Ancestor of Jesus' Mother Mary; listed third in descend 1 Ch. 8:18-10. from Zerubbabel Lu. 3:26.27.
Joed.	God is witness. Benjamite whose descndant Sallu was postexillic resident of Jerusalem Ne. 11:4.7.
Joel.	God is God. Descendants of Issachar & family head in his tribe 1 Ch. 7:1.4.

Jo-e-lah.	On of the warrios who come to David at Ziklag son of Jeroham of Gedor. 1 Ch. 12:1.
Jo.e.zer.	God is help one of the warriors joined David at Ziklag when he was still under restriction due to Saul; Karahite. 1 Ch. 12:1.2.6.
Jogli.	May God uncover reveal. A Danite whose son Bukki was chieftain of the tribe of Dan for dividing up the land of Canaan Nu. 34, 18.22-29.
John.	John is Jehohanan mean God has shown faver John the Baptiz. Son of Zechariah & Elizabeth.
Joarib.	Short from Jehoiarib. May God has conducted.
Jokim.	Short from of Jehoiakim. Propably mean God raises descendants of Judah through his third son Shelah. 1 Ch. 2:3.4:21.22.
Jokmeam.	Jok.me.am. Let the people raise up an Ephraimite City give to the Kohathites. 1 Ch. 6.66.68 at Joshua. 21:22. Jokmeam is evidently calld Kibzaim.
Jokshan.	Mean lay a snare. Descandant of Abraham by Keturah; the progenitor of Sheba and Dedan. Ge. 25:1.3; 1 Ch. 1:32.
Jonah.	Deve. Son Amitai; prohet of God from Gath-helper 2 Ki 14
Jonathan.	God has given. Englis name Jonathan. Hebrew name Yohna.than. Levite who served as priest in connection with false worship at hous of Micah in Ephraim.

Jori.	Jori. Descendan of God who is mentioned in a genealogical listing along with other head of the hous of their forefather 1 Ch. 5:11.13.15.
Joram.	Short from of Jehoram mean God is high. Son of King Toi of Hamath. Joram was sent with costly gifts made of gold, silive & copper along with his father. Congratulations to King David.
Jorim.	Descendant of King David through Nathan & an ancestor of Jesus Mother Mary, Lu. 3:23.29-31. Jarim may have lived while Uzziah was king of Judah.
Jorkeam.	Apparently a Judan site fathered; or founded by Raham. Ch. 22:44.
Josech.	Forefathe of Jesus Mother Mary. Josech was a distant descendant of David through Nathan, & the forth generation after Zerubbabel. Placing him at about the end of the Hebrew scripture era Lu. 3:23.26.27.31.
Joseph.	Short of Josiphiah mean. May God add increase added the first of Jacobs two sons by his beloved wife Rachel. Rechel Ge. 35.24.
Joshaphat.	Short of Jehoshaphat mean God is judge. One of David's warriors. A Mitnite 1 Ch. 11:26.43.
Joshbekashah.	Propably in wham affliction remains head of the 17th group of musicians at God hous son Hemon 1 Ch. 25.1???
Joshua.	Jus ha. Short of Jehosua mean God is salvtion son of Nun an Ephraimite who mustered to Moses & was later appointed ash is succeser. Ex. 33:11.

Josiah	Jo-si.ah. Related to an Arabic root May God healed son of Judean King Amon by Jedidah the daughter of Adaiah 2K 22:1.
Jotham.	God is perfect descendant of Judah designated as son of Judah 1 Ch. 2:47.
Jozacar.	God has remembered a servant of King Jahoosh of Judah.
Jubal.	Propably Ram son Leamech & Adah. Descendant of Cain.
Jubiler.	The year following each cycle of seven 7 years periods conting from Israel's entery into the promised land the Hebrew word you-vel or you-vel mean Rams horn & this refers to the suonding of Ram horn during that 50 years to proclim librty throghout the land. Le 25:9.10.
Judahs	From name Judah.
Jude.	Frome name Judah. Slave of Jesus Christ, but brother of James.
Judge.	Man rised up by God to deliver his people prior to the perior of Israel human king were kown as Judges Jg. 2:16. Moses as meditiar of the law covenant & God appointed leader.
Judith.	Feminine from of Judah a wife of Esau; daughter of Beer the Hittite & constant source of bitterness to Isaac and Rebelah. Ge. 26:34.35.

Julia.	Member of congeregation at Rome to whom Paul sent greetings Ro. 16.15. Julia my have been the wife or sister of Philologus.
Julius.	Roman army officer or centurion of the band of Augustus in whose coustody Paul traveled to Rome AC. 27.1.
Juniper.	Hebrew, berohsh. The Hebrew term for this tree his been given varios mean, such as fir tree Cypres.
Jushab.	Hesed Ju Shab-he sed one of Zerubbal's sons Ch. 3:19.20.
Kabzeel.	Kab ze eel. God has collected city in southern part of Judah. Jos. 15:21.
Kadesh.	Holy place Kadesh. In Assyrian kodshah.
Kadmiel.	God confronte; God goes in front. A Levite returning to Jerusalem with Zerubbal.
Kadmonites.	Kad monites. Mean east. A people lested among other nation whose lands God promised to Abraham's seed Ge. 15:18-21.
Kain.	Kain. Mean produce; acuire. Buy nam employed in proverbial utterance - of Balaam to refer to tribe of Kenites. Nu. 24:22.
KAIWAN.	Kai wan - apparently a star-god. As indicated by the fact that the name Kaiwan is put in a paralleilism withe the star of your god Am 5:26 Evidently the

Akkadian star Kaimanu of Kaiwan is mean since this occurs in Akkadah inscription as the nam of Saturn a star - god.

Kalali.   Priest in the days of the high prist Joiakim. He was the heas of the paternal house of Sallai. Ne. 12:12:20

Kamon.   Ka.mon. The burial place of Juge Jair. Jg. 10:15.

Kareah.   Bald. Bald. Baldness. Man of Judahs whose Johanan & Jonathan were chief of military forces in Judah.

Kedar.   Mean be dark. One of the 12 sons of Ishmael Ge. 25:13-15, 1 Ch. 1:29-31.

Kedemah.   Eastward; toward the east. Son of Ishmael named last order of Genesise. 25:15 & Chronicles 1:31

Kedemoth.   Mean east.

Kelalah.   Another name for the Levite Kelita a contempoary of Ezra the priest. Ezra. 10:23.

Kenan.   Mean produce; acquire; buy. The son of Enoch grandson of Seth.

Kenaz.   One of the sons of Esau's son Eliphaz & a Sheik in the land of Edom. Ge. 36:11.15.42.43.

| Keturah. | Kellie.tu.rah. Mean make sacrificial smoke a wife of Abraham & the mother of his six sons. Zimran Jokshan. Medon. Isbak. & Shuah ancestor of various North Arabian people dwelling to the south & east of Palestine. |

Keturah. Kellie.tu.rah. Mean make sacrificial smoke a wife of Abraham & the mother of his six sons. Zimran Jokshan. Medon. Isbak. & Shuah ancestor of various North Arabian people dwelling to the south & east of Palestine.

Kish. Merarite Levite who was the son of Mahili & brother Eleazar died without son's, having only daughters the sons of Kish.

Kittim. Is listed as one of the four sons of Javan.

Kohath. The second named of the three son of Levi Ge. 46:11. Ex. 6:16. 1 Ch. 6:1, and father of Amram. Izhar. Hebron & Uzziel Ex. 6:18. Nu. 3:19. 1 Ch. 6.2.

Kolaiah. Father of the false prophet Ahab who was among the Jews in Babylonian exille before Jerusalem destuction in 607 B.C. Jer. 29:21.

Koz. A descendant of Judah Koz be come father to Anub & Zabebah & the family Aharhel the son of Harum 1 Ch. 4:1.8.

Kushaiah. Levite of the family of Merari & the father or ancestor of Ethan.

Laadah. Descendant of Judah & the second named of Shelohs two sons. He is referred to as father of Mareshah 1 Ch. 4:21.

Laban. The grandson of Abraham brother Nahor be was the son of Betuel & brother of Rebekah. Ge. 24:15.29.28

Lael.   Belong to God. A Levite & the father of Eliasaph the

Lehad.   A descendant of Judah & the second name of Jahath two sons 1 Ch. 4:1.2.

Lahmi.   May Bread the brother of Goliath the Gittite.

Laish.   Laish, Lian.anan from Calim. The father of Patti Paltiel to whom Saul gave as
             wife his daughter Michal, previously the wife of David. Isa. 25:44, 2 Sa. 3:15.

Lamech.   The son Metushael & descendant of Cain. Ge. 4:17.18.

Lazarus.   Propably the Gr from of the Hebrew. Name Eleazar mean God has helped the
             brother of Mary & Martha.

Lebanah.   Le ba nah white full moon founder of family whose sons or descendant were among
             the Nethinim returning with Zerubbabl frorm Babylonian exille Ezra. 2:1.2.43.45.

Lebanon.   Leb-a.non. White mountain. Generaly the westernmost of the two ranges
             formin mountain system of Lebanon.

Lecah.   Le cah. Propably descendant of Judah throgh Er. 1 Ch. 4:21.

Lehabim.   Le.ha.bim - name appearing at Genesis 10:13 and Chronical, 1:11 among
             descendant of Ham through Mizraim. Since the Hebrew name is plural from,
             many scholars had that a tribe takin its name from one of Mizraim's son's is
             meant.

Livi.   Le.vi. Adherence, joined. Jacob's third son by his wife Leah - born in Paddan-
               aram Ge. 35.23.25-26.

Libni.   Mean. Whit. Grandson of Levi & the son of Gershon Gershom Ex. 6.17. 1 Ch.
               6:17. He was the founder of a family Levitical. Nu. 3:18.21.

Libya.   Aneinet Libya have been designated by Hebrew term Luvem. 1 Ch. 12:3
               Libyans old name for Libya. Phut.

Likhi.   Propably from root mean take tribe of Manassah who is name third in the list
               of Shemida's sons. 1 Ch. 7:19.

Lily.   The Hebrew term shu-shan. Lily a great variety of flower.

Lo-Ammi.   Lo-am-mi. Not my people. The name of the second son born by Hoseas wife
               Gomer.

Lois.   Lo is. Timothy's grandmother & apparently the mother of his mother
               Eunice.

Lo-ruhamah.   Lo-ru-ha-mah. She was not shawn mercy. A giral borne; by Gomer the wife of
               Hosea. Gad told the prophet to give the child this name becaus he would no
               more show mercy again to the hous of Israel.

Lot, 1.   The casting of lots is an ancient custom for deciding guestion at issue.

Lotan.	Son of Seir the Horite & one of the Sheiks of Edom. Ge. 36:20.29. His son were Hori & Herran & his sister was name Timna Ge. 36:20. 1 Ch. 1.38.39.
Lucius.	Mean light; illumintion man of Cyrene who was assciated with the Antioch Syria.
Maacah.	Ma.a.cah. The name several person of kingdom, mean squeeze. Chiled born to Nahor, Abraham's brother by his concubine Reumah. Its inhabitans derived their name from this person Ge. 22:25,24.
Maadai.	Short of Maadiah. An Israelite among the son's of Bani.
Maadiah.	God deck himself. A priest & head of paternal hous accompanying those returning from Babylonian with Zerubbable Ne. 12:1.5. Moadiah mentioned at Nehemiah. 12:17. My be the person.
Maasai.	Propably short from of Maaseiah. Priest & descendant of Immer who returned from Babylonian exile 1 Ch. 9:10.12.
Maasciah.	Work of God. Levite musician the second division who played stringed instrument. When the ark of God was brough from the hous of Obededom to Jerusalem in the David Day. 1 Ch. 15:17.20.25.
Maath.	One of Jesus ancestor listed in his genaelogy given by Luke Lu. 3:23.26.
Maaz.	Short from Ahimaaz one of Judah's descendant through Jeramee and Ram 1 Ch. 2:3.25.27.

Maaziah.	God is stronghold. Descendant of Aaron who was made head of the 24 course of priest in Davids day 1 Ch. 24:1.18.
Machi.	Machi propably short from of Machir. Gadite and the father of Geud. One of the 12 Israelite sent to spy out Canaan Ne. 13:1.2.15.16.
Machir.	Ma chir from a root mean sell. The first named son of Manasseh by his Syrian concubine. Machir founded. The family of Machirites & is called the father of Gilead.
Machirites.	Belong to Machir family of the tribe Menasseh founded by his son Machir. Nu. 26:29.
Madai.	The thierd listed son of Japheth Ge. 10:2; 1 Ch. 1:15.
Madmenah.	From a root mean manure. A site in the path of the Assyrian advance toward Jeeruslame. Isa. 10:24.31.32.
Magdiel.	Choic things of God - descendant of Esau & one of Sheiks of Edom. Ge. 36.40-43. 1 Ch. 1:51.54.
Magog.	Son of Japheth and grandson of Noah.
Mahalalel.	Propable praise of God. Descendant of Seth through Enosh and Kenan; great grandson Mahalalel lived 895 years. Ge. 5:6-17. Ch. 1:1.2.

Mahalath.   Ishmael's daughter. The sister of Nebaioth & one of the women Esau took as wife Ge. 28:9.

Mahlah.   Grow weak; fall sick. One of the daughter of Zelophehad of the tribe of Manasseh.

Mahorai.   Mean. Hurry. A might man of David military force & a Netophathite. 2 Sa. 23:8.28. 1 Ch. 11:26.30. He was descendant of Zerah.

Mahlah.   Mean. Grow weak. One of the daughter of Zelophehad of the tribe of Manasseh.

Mahli.   Mean. Grow weak. Levi grandson a son of Merari & brother of Mushi Ex. 6:16.19. 1 Ch. 6.19.29.28, Mahli was the father of Elezar & Kish.

Malcam.   Their king - Benjamite & son of Shaharaim by his wife Hodesh. 1 Ch. 8:1.8.9.

Malchiel.   Mal-chiel. God is king. My king is God grandson of of Asher & son of Beriah Ge. 46.17. He is called the father of Birzaith. 1 Ch. 7:31.

Malchijah.   May king is God. A Levi who descendant from Gershom & who an ancster of Levit musician Asaph. 1 Ch. 6:30-43.

Malchiram.   Mal.chi.ram. My king is high one of the sons of King Jecaniah. Jehoiachin as a prisoner in Babylon 1 Ch. 3.17,18.

Malchishua.   May king hears my one king Saul sons Isa. 14:49; 1 Ch. 8:33.9.39.

Malchus.   Mean king-high priest's slave who accompanied Judah Iscariot & the crowd to Gethsemane.

Mallothi.   Mean. Make signs; Utter, Akohathite, Levite & one the 14 sons of singer Heman 1 Ch. 25:4.5.

Malluch.   Mean reign as king or king. Meranite Levi and forefather of the Levitical singer Ethan 1 Ch. 6:44.47.

Man.a.en.   One who comforts man who was anmong the prophets & teacher in the congregation at Antioch. He had been educated with the district ruler Herod. Antipas Ac 13:1.

Manahath.   Mean - reast; settledown. Descendant of Seir through Shobal. Ge. 36.20.23. 1 Ch. 1:38.40.

Manahathites.   Belog Manahath certain Judean descendant from Caleb and Salma who apparently constituted part of the population of Mahahath 1 Ch. 2:50.51.

Manasseh.   One making forgetful; one who makes forget Joseph's first born son a grandson of Jacb.

Manoah.   Danite man of the Shephelah town of Zorah Jos: 15:33 and the father of Judge SAmsan.

Maoch.   Father of Achish of the Philistine city Cath.

Markt.   The Roman of the son of Mary of Jerusalem.

Maresena.   One of seven princes consulted by Ahasuerus on Vasht's refusel to obey Es.
               1:14.

Martha.   Jewess, the sister of Lazarus and Mary of Bethany Joh. 11:1.2.

Mash.   Descendant of Shena through Aram. Ge. 10:22.23. 1 Ch. 1:17.

Mattan.   Ancestor of Joseph - Mattan Joseph grandfather. Mt. 1:15.16.

Matthat.   Short from Mattithia mean gift of God.

Mebunnai.   Mighty man in Davids army Ahushothite man in Davids army a Hushathite
               2 Sa. 23.27.

Medan.   One of Abraham's six son's by his wife concubine Keturah. Ge. 25:1.2. 1 Ch.
               1:32.

Mehetabel.   God does good. Daughter of woman matred & wife of Edomite King Hadad
               Ge. 36:31.39. 1 Ch. 1:50.

Mehida.   Ancstor of family of Nehinim whose son's or descendant returned to Judah
               from Bablonian exile with Zerubbabel in 537 B.C. Ezr. 2:1.43.52. Ne. 7:54.

Mehujael.	Struck by God. Great-grandson of Cain was the father of Methushel & grandfather of Lamech Ge. 4:17.18.
Melech.	King. One of the sons of Mich & a descendant of Kink Saul of Israel. Great-grandson of Saul son Jonathan 1 Ch. 33.35. 9:39.41.
Meonathai.	Descendant of Judah. Becom father to Ophrah.
Mepbib.o. sheth.	One of King Saul's two 8ons by Rizpah the daughter of Aiah 2 Sa. 21:8.
Meraioth.	Me.ra.ioth propably. Rebellious ones. Priestly descendant of Aaron through Eleazers called the son of Zerphiah. 1 Ch. 6:3-7.52. Ezr. 7:3.4.
Merari.	Mean be bitter. Son of Levi & brother of Gershon & Kohath. Ge 46:11. 1 Ch. 6:1.16.
Mered.	Son of Ezra. Mered had an Egyptian wif Bithiah the daughter of pharaoh by whom Mered had sons 1 Ch. 4:1.17.18.
Meremoth.	One of the head priest acompanying Zerubbal from Babylon to Jerusalem in 537 B.C. - Ne. 12:1.7.
Meres.	One of the seven princes whom Ahasuerus consulted when Veshti disobeyed him Ex. 1:14.

Merdodach-Baladan.	Mer.o.dach-bal.a.dan. from Babylonian Marduk has given a son. The son of Baladan & king of Babylon who sent letter & a gift to King Hezekih of Judah following that king recovery from illness Isa. 39:1. He is called Berodach-baladan at Kings 20:12.
Mesha.	Fistborn son of Caleb the son of Hezron tribe of Judah. Mesha was father or founder of Ziph. 1 Ch. 2:18.42.
Meshach.	Me-shach the Babylonian name given by Nebuchadnezzars chief court official to Daniels companion Mishael. The mean of this new name is uncertian but it may have have included a reference to <u>Aku</u>. A Sumerian god.
Meshelemiah.	Me-shel-e-mi-ah. God makes peace. Kohathite Levit & ancestral head of Divison of Korahites.
Meshezabel.	Man of Judah - of the family of Zerah & whose son Pethahahiah was at the side of king for every matter of the peace. Ne. 11:24.
Meshullemeth.	Me.shul.le.meth. The feminine form of Meshull-am. Daughter of Haruz from Jotbah who become the wife of Judean King Manasseh & mother of King Amon. 2 Ki. 21:19.20.
Mesopotamia.	Mes-o-po-ta-mia. From Gr-meaning land between rivers. The Greek term for the strech located between the Tigrs and Euphrates rivers.
Messiah.	Mean anointed or anointed one. Mt. 2:4.

Methushael.	Me.thu.sha.el. Man of God. Descendant of Cain through Enoch. Methushael was the son of Mehujael and the father of Lamech. Not to be confused with Noah's father Lamech Ge. 4:17.18.
Micah.	Book of a prophetic book of Hebrew scriptures containing God word through Samaria & Jerusalem. Mic. 1:2.3.1.6:1.
Michal.	King Saul's younger daughter who becom wife of David.
Midian.	Midianites. Belong to Midian. One of Abrahams son's by concubine Keturah. The fathe of Ephah. Epher Hanoch, Abida and Eldaah. Ge. 25:1.2.4 Ch. 1:32.33.
Mijamin.	From the right hand. Descendant of Aaron selected by Lot to head the six divison of priesty service in King David day. 1 Ch. 24:1.3.5.9.
Mikloth.	Mik.loth. Father of Shimeah. Shimeam of the Benjamite Jeiel of Gibeon 1 Ch. 8:1.29.32.9.35.38.
Milalai.	Mil.a.lai. Levite musician who marched in on of the inaugural procession on Jerusalem rebult wall in Nehemiahs day. Ne. 12:31.36.
Milcom.	From root mean king. The same as Molech. God of the Amonities.
Milcah.	Mil.cah. Daughter of Abraham.
Millo.	Mil.lo mean fill the house of Milla. Beth Millo.

Mina.	Mi.na. Unit both weigh & of monetary value 1 Ki. 10; 17. Ezra. Ne. 7:71 according to the Hebrew text Ezekiel. 45.12.
Miniamin.	Right hand. One of the Levites serving under Kare in office of trust for the distribution of the holy contribution among their brother at priests cites in King Hezekiahs day 2 Ch. 31:14.15.
Mishael.	Propably. Who belongs to God. Kohathite Levite and son of Uzziel. Ex. 6:18.22.
Mishma.	Mish.ma. Son of Ishmael. Ge. 25:14.16. 1 Ch. 1.30:31 Simeonite, son of Mibsam & father of Hammuel. 1 Ch. 4:24.26.
Mispar.	Propably Nuber leadin person the Jews returning with Zerubbabel from Babyonian exile. Ezra. 2:1-2. He is called Mispereth at Nehemiah 7:???
Mizpah.	Mean watchtower. Region inhabited by Hirite & situeated at the base of Mount Herman was known as the Land of Mizpah Jos. 11:3.
Mizraim.	Second son of Ham Ge. 10:6.
Mizzah.	Sheik of Edom a descendant of Esau through Reuel Ge. 36:17. 1 Ch. 1:34-37.
Mnason.	Native of Cyprus & an early disciple Paul.
Moab.	Moabites. Son of Lot by his older daughter.

Moladah.   Mother.la.dah. Mean give birth become father to bear one of the cities in southern Judah allotted to Simon.

Molech.   Mean reign as king.

Molid.   Mo.lid. Mean give birth. Become father to bear. Man of Judah & desndat of Hezron through Jerahmeel. Molid was the son of Abishur by his wife Abihail 1 Ch. 2:4.5.9.25-29.

Mordecai.   Mor.de.cai. One who returned to Jerusalem & Judah in 537 B.C. after the 70 years of exile in Babylon. Ezra. 2:1.2.

Moza.   Going forth descendant of Judah & son of Caleb by his concubin Ephah. 1 Ch. 2:46.

Muppim.   One of the sons of Benjamin Ge. 46:21. Evidently with Shephuphan Ne. 26:21. Shephuphan. 1 Ch. 8:5 and Shuppim. 1 Ch. 7:12.

Mushi.   Grandson of Levi & son of Merari Ex. 6:16.19. Mushi become father to three sons and founded a family called the Mushite 1 Ch. 23:23. Nu. 26:58.

Naam.   Pleasant. Son of Caleb, Jephunneh's son of tribe of Judah. 1 Ch. 4:1.15.

Naamah.   Pleasant. Descendant of Cain; sister of Tubal-Cain and the daugh of Lameh by Zillah. Ge. 4:17-19.22.

Naaman.	Mean. Be pleasnt. Grandson of Benjamin through his firstborn Bela. 1 Ch. 8:1-4.7.
Naarai.	Na.a.rai. Propably short from of Neariah mean boy young man of son of Ezbal & mighty man in Davids military forces 1 Ch. 11:26.37.
Nabonidus.	From Babylonian mean Nebo Baylonin God is exalted last supreme monarch of the Babylonin Empire; father of Belshazzar on the basis of cuneiform texts he is believed to have ruled some 17 years 556-539 B.C. He was given to literature, art and religion.
Naham.	Na.ham. Comfort brother in law of Hodiaha descendant of Judah. 1 Ch. 4:1.19
Nahamani.	Mean comfort. One who returned with Zerubbabel from Babylonin exle. Ne. 7.6.7.
Naharai.	Na-ha-r. Beerthithite & one of Joabs armor-bearers. Naharal was among the mighty men of David miltary force. 2 Sa. 23:24.37, 1 Ch. 11:26.39.
Nahash.	Na.hash. Serpent. King of the Arnmonites at the time Saul began his reign Nahash brought his army aginst Jabesh in Gilead.
Nahath.	Na.hath. Rest. Shik of Edom. Son of Reuel & Grandson of Esau & his wife Basemaths daughter. Ge. 36:2-4.
Nahshon.	Nah.shon. Mean serpent. Wilderness chieftain of the tribe of Judah. Nahshon was the son of Amminadab & among the fifth-listed generation after Judah. 1 Ch. 2:3-10. His sister was Aarons wife Ex. 6:23.

Nahum.	Na.hum. Comforter that is an encourage. Israelite prophet of the seventh century B.C. & the writer at the book bearing his name Nahum have been in Judah at the time he recorded his prophecy. Na. 1:15.
Naphtali.	My wrestlings. The second son born to Jacob by Rachels maidservant Bilhah in Paddan-aram Ge. 35:25.26. Ex. 1:1.4. 1 Ch. 2:1.2.
Nard.	The precious perfumed oil that Mary the sister of Lazarus appiled to Jesus head & feet by reason of its constliness. Nard Gr.nar.dos.
Nathan.	God has given father of Zabad. Nathan's grandfather was an Egyptian servant named Jerha 1 Ch. 2:3.34-36.
Neariah.	Ne.a.ri.ah. Boy young man Simeonite. Son of Ishi. Neariah and his three brother.
Ne.bat.	He has looked at. Ephraimit and father of King Jeroboam/ the first ruler of the ten-tribe kingdom of Israel 1 Ki 11.26; 2 Ki. 14:23.24.
Nedabiah.	God is willing. Son of King Jeconiah. Born during Jeconiah exile in Babylon. 1 Ch. 3:17.18. 2 Ki. 24:15.
Nehushta.	Daughter of Elnathan of Jerusalem & wife of king when the first captive were thaken to Babylon in 617 B.C.
Ne.ko.da.	Speckled the forfather of a grup of Nethinim who returned from Babylonian exile in 537 B.C. Ezr. 2:1 43.48. Ne. 7:46.50.

Nemuel.	First of Simeon's five sons & family head of the Nemuelites. Nu. 26:12-14. 1 Ch. 4:24.
Ne.phag.	Son of Izhar & brother of Korah & Zichri of the tribe of Levi. He was cousin of Moses and Aaron. Ex. 6:16.18.
Nephusheim.	Nephusim. A family head of Nephinim some of whose descendants returned returned from Babylonian exile with Zerubbabel 537 B.C. Ne. 7:6.7.46.52 Ezr. 2:43.
Ner.	Lamp. Benjamite. Son of Abiel. Jeiel fathe of Abner & Kish & grandfather of King Saul. Isa. 14:50.51.
Nethanel.	Ne.than.el God has given. Chieftain of the tribe of Issachar; son of Zuar Nu. 1:18.16.
Nethinim.	Neth.i.nim. Given Ones. Non Israelites temple slaves or ministers 1 Ch. 9:2, Ezr. 8:17.
Neziah.	Mean. Oversee. Forefather of a group of Nethinime who returned with Zerubbale after the Babylonian exile 537 B.C. Eza. 2:1-2.43.54.
Ni.ger.	Ni.ger. from Lot, mean dark black. The Latin.
Nile.	The Greek nam given to the river.
Nimrah.	Mean. Tiger.

Nimrod.	Son of Cush. 1 Ch. 1:110. Name of Nimrod. He stirred up the whole world to rebel. That way been called Nimrod.
Nimshi.	Nim.shi. Father of Jehoshaphat. Not the king & grandfather of God 1 Ki. 19:16. 2 Ki. 9:2:14. 2 Ch. 22:
Nineveh.	City of Assyria. Founded by Nimrod. A mighty hunter in opposition to God. The gredd city. Ge. 10:9.11.12.
No.a.mon.	Egypt mean city of Amon an amon god.
Noah.	Noah. Rest. Son of Lamech. Heb. No.ach. Rest.
Nobah.	No.bah. Mean bark. Israelite probably of the tribe of Manasseh. He named the city after himself. Nu. 32:42.
Nogah.	Mean shine. Son of King David born to Jerusalem 1 Ch. 3:5-7.14.3-6.
Noah.	Mean rest; settle down. The fourth son of Banjamin. 1 Ch. 8:1.2.
Noph.	The usual Hebrew scripture name for Memphis. An important city of ancient Egypt. Isa. 19:13. Jer. 2:16.44.1.46. Ezra. 30.13.
Nun.l.	Father of Moses' successor Joshua; son of Elishama of the tribe of Ephraim. Ex. 33:11 1 Ch. 7:20.26.27.

Obadiah.	Servan of God. Family head of Issachar son of Izrahiah & descendant of Tola. 1 Ch. 7.1-3.
Obadiah.	Book of. Book of Prophet Obadiah.
Obal.	The 8th son of Joktan's 13 sons. Descendant of Sham.
Obed.	O.bed. servant. Descendant of Judah. The father of Jehu & the son of Ephlal of the family of Jerahmeel. 1 Ch. Ch. 2:3.25.37.38.
Obed-Edom.	Mean. Servant of Edom. Gittite at whose home the Ark of the Covenat was kept for three month after its near upset & the accompaying death of Uzzah for duration of its stay there there Obed-edom & his houshold were blessed by God.
Obil.	Ishmaelite caretaker of Davids camels. 1 Ch. 27.30.
Ohad.	The third-listed son of Simeon Ge. 46:10. Ex. 6.15.
Ohel.	Tent. Son of Governor Zerubbal & descendant of David. 1 Ch. 3:19.20.
OG.	Amorite king of Bashan 1 Ki. 4:19. Og was one of the giant Rephim.
Oholibamah.	Tent of the high place Canaanite wife of Esau. She bore him three sons. Jalam. Jeush & Korah. All become Shieks of Edom.

Omar.	Mean. Say second son of Esau's. First born Eliphaz a Shiek of Edom Gen. 36:10.11.15. 1 Ch. 1:36.
Omer.	A dry measure amounting to one tenth of an Ephah Ex. 16:16.18.22.32.
Ophir.	Descandant of Sham through Arpachshad Shelah. Eber and Joktan. Ge.10:22.29.
Ophrah.	Descendant of Judah through Meonothai. 1 Ch. 4:1.14.
Oren.	Son of Jerahmeel in the tribe of Judah. 1 Ch. 2:25.
Oreb.	O.rab. Raven. Prince of Midian Oreb & Zeeb were in the Midianite army of Kings Zebah & Zalmunna that Gideon & his 300 put to fight the two prices. Jg. 7:24.25.8.3.5. Ps. 8:3.4.
Ornan.	Or.nan. Jebusite from whom Divd bought the threshing floor that later become the site for the templ. 1 Ch. 21:18-28. 2 Ch. 3:1. Ornan is also called Araunoh.
Orpah.	Or.pah. The Moabite wife of Chillion & like Ruth. A daughter in law of Naom.
Othni.	Short of Othnie son Shemaiah of Korahite Obededom appointed as a Levite gatekeeper befor the sanctuary. 1 Ch. 26:1.4.6-8.15.
Othniel.	The firs name judge of Israel after Joshua. Othniel was the son of Kenaz. Caleb's younger brother. Jg. 1:13.3.9. Jos 15:17.

Ozem.	O.zem. Fourth son of Jeraheel in the tribe of Judah. 1 Ch. 2:25.
Ozni.	Probably short from of Azaniah. Son of Gad & founder of the tribal family of Oznites numbered in the Second Wilderness registration of Israel Nu. 26:15.16. Ozni called Ezbon in the first of Gad's son's som of names writen differently.
Paarai.	Papably meaning open wide one of mighty men of Davids military forces 2 Sa 23:8.35.
Padon.	Mean. Redeem paternal head of a family of Nethinim. The son of Padon returned with Zerubbabl from Babylon exile Ezra. 2:1.43.44. Ne. 7:46.47.
Pagiel.	Pa.gi.el. Encounter with God Wilderness chieftain of the tribe of Asher. Son of Ochram Nu. 1:13.16.
Palal.	Short of Pelaliah. Repairer of section of Jerusalem. Wall in the days of Nehemiah son of Uzai Ne. 3:25.
Palestine.	Pa.lai.sti.ne. Son of Casluim. Sea people from Agen Sea. The defeated by Mesraim many times. They call them sea people.
Paltite.	Pal.tite. Pelang to Pelet or of belong to hous of Pelet. One of Davids mighty men. & refer to native of Bethe-Pelet. 2 Sa 23:8.26.
Palti.	Short from the Paltiel.a Banjamite chieftan selected as on of the 12 spies to preview the Land of Canaa in 1512 B.C. He was son of Raphu Nu. 13.2.3.9.

Paltiel.	Pal.tie.el. God is my provider of Escpe reibresentative of Issachar at the time the tribe divieded the promised land into inheritance portions; son of Azzan Nu 34:17.18.26.
Parnch.	Zebulunite whose son Elizapn was the tribal representative in dividing the promised land. Nu. 34:17.18.25.
Parshandatha.	Par.shan.da.tha. from Perian. Probaly mean the investigator. One of Hamans ten son's. Ezra. 9:7.
Parthians.	Belong to Parthia. Jews & proselytes from Parthia are listed first among those visitor attending the Festival of Pentecost. 33. C.E. in Jerusalem. God Gods Holy Sepirt poured out one group of about 120 Christian disciples enabled them to proclaim the good news in the language or dialect of those Parthians. Ac. 1:15.2.1.4-12.37-47.
Paul.	Little; small. Israelite of the tribe of Benjamine & an apostle of Jesus Christ Eph. 1:1. Php. 3:5. Perhaps having both the Hebrew nam Saul & Roman name Paul from childhood Ac. 9:17. 2 Pe 3:15.
Pedahel.	God has redeem chieftain of Naphtali. Nu. 34.16.
Pedahzur.	The rock has redeem man in the tribe of Manasseh.
Pelaiah.	God has acted wonder. Levite who assisted Ezra in reading & explaining the law to Israelites assembled in Jerusalem.

Peleg.   Division. Son of Eber father of Reu.

Pelet.   Providing of escape. Son of Dahdai in the Calebite division of Judah's genealogy. 1 Ch. 2:47.

Peniel.   Pe.ni.el. The place or near the ford of the Jabbo where Jacob wrestled with angel henc he called the pleace Paniel because there he had seen God face to face Ge. 32:22-31. The Sam as Penuel.

Peninah.   Cora. Wife of Elkanah.

Penuel.   Pe.nu.el. Face of God. Father of Cedor in tribe of Judah 1 Ch. 4:1.4.

Peresh.   Pe.resh. Son of Machir & Maach in the tribe of Manasseh 1 Ch. 7:14.16.

Pethar.   The hom of Bahaam. The prophet who to cures Israel Pethor was situated by river. Apparently the Euphrates in Aram-Naharaim Masoretic text or Moesopotamia Nu. 22:5.23.7. De. 23:4. It is generly indentified with the Pitru of Assyrian inscription. Pitru lay on the Sajur River.

Pethuel.   Father of the prophet. Joe. 1:1.

Peullethai.   Mean. Wages. The eighth of Obed-edom's sons listed as a gatekeeper. 1 Ch. 26:1.4.5.15.

Phanuel.   Hebrew. Penuel mean face of God. Descendant of Asher who daughter Anna was a prophess at the teple in Jeruslem when Joseph & Mary brought Jesus there. Luke. 2:36.

Pharisees.   Prominent relgios Sect of Judaism existing in the first century.

Phicol.   Army chief of Philistine King Abimelech.

Philemon.   Loving a Christian slave owner associated with the congregation at Colossea.

Philip.   Mean fond of horses. Horse loving. One of earliest disciples among the 12 apostles of Jesus Christ.

Phlegon.   Burning one of the Roman Christian whom Paul greets in his letter. Ro. 16:14.

Phoenicia.   Mean. Palem tree. For many years the principl city of ancient Phoenicia was Sidon. But later it was eclipsed in importance by Tyre. A city founded by colony from Sidan.

Pinon.   One of the Sheik of Esau Edom. Ge. 36:40-43. 1 Ch. 1:51.

Pishon.   Propably more scattered one of the four rivers branching out from the river issuing ut of Edan Ge. 2:10-12.

Pithon.   Descendant of King Saul through Jonathan & Merb-baal Mephibo Sheth. 1 Ch. 8:33-35.9.39.41.

Pochereth-Hazzebim.	Po.che.reth. Haz.zebim. Head of a family whose descendant were among the sons of the servants of Solomon returnin from exile under the leadership of Zerubbable. Ezr. 2:1.2.55. Ne. 7.59.
Potiphar.	Poti.phar. from Egyptian. A shortened from of Potiphera. An Egyptian court official & chief of Pharaoh's bodyguard. He was a Joseph's master for time ???. It appear. Was aman. Wealth. Ge. 37.36.39.4.
Potiphera.	Pot.i.phe.ra. Egyptian. Mean. He whom Ra has given. Joseph's father in law. Whose daughter Asenath bore Manasseh & Ephram Ge. 41:45.50.46.20.
Prisca.	Old woman: Priscilla. Pris.cil.la.Littel old woman. Shorter from of the name is found in Paul's writings, the longer from Luke's.
Puah.	Pu.ah. name represents two similar Hebrew name that differ in gende and mean but that are sepelled alike in both their Grek & English translation. Pu.ah second son of Issachar. 1 Ch. 7:1.
Pul.	The name given a king of Assyria as 2 Kings. 15:19. 1 Ch. 5:26. During the reign of Menahem King of Israel. Pul entered Palestine & received tribute from Menahem.
Purah.	Pu.rah. The attendant. Probably armor bearer, of Gideon who went with him during the night to spy on the Midianite camp. Jg. 7:9-15.
Puthites.	Family that lived in Shobal - 1 Ch.2:52.53.

Putiel.	Pu.ti.el. Father in law of Aaron's son Eleazar & grandfather of Phinehas. Ex. 6.25.
Puvah.	Son of Issachar whose family descendant were called Punites Ge. 46:13. Nu. 26:23. His name is sepelled Puah at 1 Chronicle. 7:1.
Quirinius.	Qui.rin.i.us. Roman governer of Syria at the time of the registration ordered ordered by Caesar Augustus that resuleted in Jesus birth taking place in Bethlehem. Lu. 2:1.2 his full name was Publius Sulpicius Quirinius.
Raamah.	Son of Ham's first born Cush & brother of Nimrod. Raamah & his two sons Sheba & Dedan founded three of the 70 post - flood families Ge. 10:6-8. 1 Ch. 1:9.
Raamses.	Ra.am.ses. Ramises. Egyptian. Mean Ra. The sun-god has begotten him where Jacobs family moved into Egypt they were assigned to live in the land of Raameses Ge. 47:11.
Rabboni.	Semitic word mean my teacher.
Rabsaris.	Rab.sa.ris. Chief court official in Assyrian & Babylonian governments.
Rabshakeh.	Rab.sha.keh from Akkadian propbly mean Chief Cupbearer the title of a major Assyrian offical 2 Ki. 18:17.
Raddai.	Jesses fifth. Named son an older brother of David in the tribe of Judah. 1 Ch. 2:13-15.

Rahab.   Wide spacious. Prostitute of Jericho.

Raham.   Vulture. Son of Shema in the Calebite branch of Judah's genealogy 1 Ch. 2:4.5.9.42-44.

Ram.   Descendant of Judah through Perez & Hezron.

Ramathite.   Belong to Bamah. Descndant for Shimei the vineyard keeper of King David 1 Ch. 27:27.

Ramathaim-   The home of Elkanah. Father of Samuel.
Zophim.

Rapha.   Mean. Heal. Son of Benjamin. The fifth son. 1 Ch. 8:1.2.

Raphah.   Short of Rephaiah. Mean God has healed. Descendant of Benjamin through Saul. Also called Rephaiah.

Raphu.   Mean. Heal. Benjamin whose son Palti was one of the 12 to spy out the land of Canaan in 1512 B.C. Nu. 13:9.16.

Reaiah.   Re.a.iah. God has seen. Son of Shobal & descendant of Judah 1 Ch. 4:1.2.

Reba.   On of the five king of Midian slain in the avenging of Midinss immoral seduction of Israel Nu. 31:2.8.

Rech.   The tribe of Judah. 1 Ch. 4:12.

Recab.   Chairoteer. Benjamite son of Remmon the Beerathites.

Reelaiah.   One whose nam occurs with those of such prominent man as Zerbbabel & Jeshua. As those returing from Babylon to Jerusalem in 537 B.C. Ezra. 2:1.2.

Regem.   Regem. First son of Jahai in the Galebite branch of Judah's genealogy. 1 Ch. 2:3.42.47.

Rehoboam. Re.ho.bo.am. Widen make spacious the people. Son of Solomon by his Ammonite wife Naamuh.

Rei.   Re.i. Companion friend one of David's mighty me who refused to join Adonijah's conspriacy 1 Ki 1:8.

Rekem.   Weaver. A king of Midian.

Remaliah. Father of Israelite King Pekah. 2 Ki. 15:25. 2 Ch. 28.

Rephael.   God has healed. Son of Obed-dom's first Shemaiah.

Rephah.   Ephramite ancestor of Joshua 1 Ch. 7:22-27.

Rephaiah.   God has healed. Secon. Named son of Tola & head of a paternal house in the tribe of Issachar Ch. 7:1.2.

Resurrection.   The Greek word an'stasis. Mean raising.

Reu.   Companion; friend. Son of Pleg & father of Serug. 1 Ch. 1:24-27.

Reuben.   Reu.ben. See, son the firstborn of Jacob's 12 son's. God has looked upon my wretchednes Ge. 29:30-32 1 Ch. 2:1.

Reuel.   Reu.el. Companian. Frined of God. Second-named son of Esau. By Ishmael's daughter Basemath. Reuele's own four son's become Edomits Shiek's. Ge. 36:2-4.10.17. 1 Ch. 1:35.37.

Reumah.   Reu.mah. Concubine of Abraham's brother Nahor. She gave birth to four sons. Ge. 22.20.24.

Rhesa.   Rhesa.son. That is descendant of Zerbbabl. Lu. 3.23.27.

Rib.bai.   Propably short from of Jeriboi mean may he contened our legal case. Benjamin of Gibeah son Ittai or Ithai was one of David's thirty famous warrior's 2 Sa. 23:24. 1 Ch. 11.31.

Rimmon.   Rim.mon. Pomegrant tree. Benjamite fathe of Baanah & Rechab. 2 Sa. 4:2.5-7.9.

Rimmon.   Pomegrante tre. Benjemit father Baanah & Rechab.

Rizia.   Mean take pleasur; approve. Warrior & family head in the tribe of Asher; son of Ulla. 1 Ch. 7:39.40.

Rohgah.   Second-listed son of Shemer in genealogy of Asher 1 Ch. 7:30.34.

RuFus.   Ru.fus. Red. Son of the Simon who was complled to help carry Jesus cross. Mr. 15.21. Lu. 23:26.

Rumah.   Ru.mah. Height; exalted place home of Zebidah & her father Pedaiah. Wife of King Joisiah of Judah and the mother of Jehoiak. 2 Ki. 23:34.36.

Ruth.   Moabite who married Boaz.

Sabteca.   Sab.te.ca. Fifth named son of Cush & father of one of the 70 post-flood families Ge. 10:7.32. 1 Ch. 1:9.

Sabeans.   Sa.be.ans. The designation of band of raider who attaked the property of Job of land of Uz.

Sacar.   Sa.car. Wages. Haraite father of David. Warrior of Ahiam. 1 Ch. 11:26.35. Sacar is caled Sharar at 2 Samuel. 23:33.

Sachia.   Sa.chi.a. The head of paternal house in the tribe Benjamin; son of Shavaraim by his wife Hodesh 1 Ch. 8:1.8-10.

Sadducees.	Sad.du.cees. A prominent religious sect. of Judaism associated with the priesthood Ac. 5:17. They did not beleve in either resurection or angeles.
Sallai.	Sal.la.i. Name in the list of Benjamites who lived in Jerusalem following the Babylonian exile Nu. 11:4.7.8.
Sallu.	Sal.lu. Benjamite resident of Jerusalem son of Meshullam. 1 Ch. 9:3.7. Ne. 11:7.
Salma.	Descendant of Judah & ancestor of David 1 Ch. 2:3-5.9-15. He is also called Salmon. Ru. 4:12.18-22. Lu. 3:32.
Salmon.	The son of Judahs chiftian Nashon.
Salome.	Sa-lo.me. Probably from Heb-mean peace.
Salu.	Simeonite whose son Zimri was executed for immorality on the plaines of Moab. Nu. 25:14.
Samgar.	Nebo. Name or title of one of Babylonian princes who enterd Jerusalem right after a breanch was made in its walls in the sumer of 607 B.C. Jer. 39.3.
Samlah.	Sam.lah. Fifth. Named king of Edom.
Sanballat.	San.bal.lat from Akkdian. Mean resident of Beth-horon or of Horonain who opposed Nehemiah Ne. 2:10.

Sapphira.	Sap.phi.ra. from Aramaic & mean beautiful the wife of Ananias with her husband. She entered conspiracy that resulted in their death.
Sarah.	Princess Sarai. Propably contentious. Half sister & wife of Abraham & mother of Isaac Ge. 11:29.20.
Saraph.	Sa.raph. Mean burn. Descendant of Shelah of the tribe of Judah. One who took a Moabite wife.
Sargon.	From old Akkadian and Assyrain mean the king is legitimate the succesor Shalmaneser as king of Assyria. Historian refer to him as Sargon II. An earlier king, not of Assyria but of Babylon is designted as Sargon 1.
Sarsechim.	Sar.se.chim. Propably chief of the slaves a Babylonian prince who was among the first to enter Jerusalem after the army broke through the walls in the sum of 607 B.C. Jer. 39.2.3.
Saul.	Asked of Lord. Inquired of God. Benjamite descendant from Jeiel & also caled Abiel through Ner and Kish 1 Ch. 8.29:33.9.35-39.
Sceva.	A Jewish chief priest his seven sons were among certain of roving Jew who practiced the casting out of demon in one instance in the city Ephesus. The tried to exorcise a demon by saying, I solemnly charge yuo by Jesus whom Paul preaches. Ac. 19:13-20.
Seah.	Se.ah. A dry measure that according to Rabbinc sources, is equel to one third of an Ephah. Ge. 18:6. Isa 25.18.

Seba.	Se.ba. One of five son of Cush. Ge. 10:7. 1 Ch. 1:9.
Sebam.	Se.bam. Apparently an alternate nam for Sibmah. Nu. 32.3.38.
Segub.	Se.gub. High up; proteted. Son of Hezron & father of Jair in the tribe of Judah. 1 Ch. 2:21.22.
Seir.	Mean bristle up. Propably refering to wood hills. A Horite whose seven sons were Shieks in the land of SEir. Prior to its being occupied by Esau. Edom. Ge. 36:20.
Selied.	Se.led. Mean leap for joy. Son of Nadab. 1 Ch. 2:25.30-85.
Sepharvites.	Belong to Sepharvaim. People of the city Sepharvaim after 740 B.C. at leat some of the inhaitans of Sepharvaim were taken by Assyrian as colonist to Samaria.
Serah.	Daughter of Asher & wife of Abraham.
Seraiah.	God has contended. Son of Kenaz in the tribe of Judah. Brother of Judge Othniel & nephew of Caleb the spy Seraiah's descendants through his son Joab becom craftsman 1 Ch. 4:13.14.
Sered.	Se.red. First son of Zebulun & founder of Seredites a Zebulunite tribal family. Ge. 46:14. Nu. 26:26.27.
Seredites.	Ser.e.dites. Belong to Sered. Zebulunite founded by Sered. Nu. 26:26.

Shaaph.   Sha.aph. Son of Caleb. Son of Hezron by his concubin Maacah Shaaph was the founder or father of those who settled Madmannah. 1 Ch. 2:9.42.

Shabbethai.   Shab.be.thai. Born on the Shbbath apostexilic.

Shagee.   Sha.gee. Hararite. Whose son Jonathan was one of David's mighty men. 1 Ch. 11:26.34.

Shaharaim.   Sha.ha.ra.im. Born of dawn. Benjamin who lived in Moab for time & whose three named wives bore him many sons. 1 Ch. 8:8-11.

Shadrash.   Sha.drach. The Babylonian nam of Jewish exile elevated to high position in the government of Babylon.

Shallum.   Mean. Make peas. Last name son of Naphtali. 1 Ch. 7:13. Spelled Shillem.

Shalman.   Mean. Make peace.

Shalmaneser.   From Akkadian. Mean Shulman an Assyrian god is superios.

Shama.   Sha.ma. Short from Shemaiah. God has heard. One of David mighty men; brother of Jeiel & son of Hotham the Aroerite. 1 Ch. 11:26.44.

Shamgar.   Sham.gar. A deliverer of Israel between the judgeships of Ehud & Barok only one heroic of Shamgar is recoreded. The slaying of 600 Philistines with cattle goad. But he is accredited thereby with saving Israel Jg. 3:31.

Shamhuth.	Sham.huth. Izrahite chifetain for the fifth month in Davids rotational service reorganization. 1 Ch. 27.8.
Shamir.	Sha.mir. Levite who was the son of Micah. Ch. 24:20.24.
Shamma.	Sham.ma. Leading member of the tribe Asher son or descendant of Zophah. 1 Ch. 7:36.37.40.
Shammah.	Sham.mah. Edomite Sheik; grandson of Esau through Reuel. Ge. 36:10.13.17. 1 Ch. 1:37.
Shammai.	Sham.mai. Mean hear. Listen. Man in the Jerahmeelite branch of Judah's genealogy; son of Onam and father of Nadab & Abishur. 1 Ch. 2:4.5.9.
Shammoth.	Sham.moth. One of Davids mighty men; a Harorite 1 Ch. 11:26.27.
Shammua.	Shamu.a. Short from of Shemaiah mean. God has heard. Listened. One of tribe Reuben whom Moses sent into the promised land as a spy. Son of Zaccur. Nu. 13:2-4.28.29.
Shamsherai.	Sham.she.rai. The head of forefather Shaus that lived in Jerusalem; son of Jeronam in the tribe of Benjamin. 1 Ch. 8:1.26-28.
Samuel	Sam.uel. Name of God. Prophet. Ac 3:24
Shaphm.	The second in charge of tribe of God in Bashan.

Shaphat.	Short of Shephatian. Mean God has judged chieftain representing the tribe of Simon one of spies who sepent 40 days in the promised land son of Hori Nu. 13:2-5.25.
Sharai.	One of those sons of Binnui who after exile.
Sharar.	Harite father of David's warrior Ahiam. 2 Sa. 23:33.
Sharezer.	Son of Assyrian King Sennacherib some time after his faths defeat by God Sharezer & his brother Adrammelech killed their father, sword whild he was bowing down to his idol god & they fled to the land of Ararat. 2 Ki. 19:7.35-37.
Sharon.	The martime plain betwen the plain of Dor & of Carmel. An the plain of Philistia.
Shashai.	Sha.shai. One of the postexilic son of Binnui who took foreign wives.
Shashak.	Benjamite whose 11 sons listed the headmen who lived in Jerusalem 1 Ch. 8:14.22-25.28.
Shaul.	Asked God. Asked of God. Sixth named king of ancient Edom; successor of Samlah of Baalhanan. Shaul was Rehobath the river Ge. 36.31.37.
Shalites.	Belong to Shaul. Simonite family founded by Shaul Nu. 26:12.13.
Shaysha.	Shay.sha. Secretary of King David. 1 Ch. 18:16.

Sheal.   She.al. One of several in the family of Bani whom Ezra induced to dismis foreign wives & sons Ezra. 10:10.11.

Shealtiel.   She.al.ti.el. Asked of God. Descendant of David & tribe of Judah.

Sheraiah.   She.a.ri.ah. Descendant of Saul & Jonathan one of Azeil's six sons. 1 Ch. 8:33-38.9:44.

Sheba.   The first-listed son of Raamah the son of Cush. Ge. 10:7. 1 Ch. 1:9.

Shebeaniah.   Sheb.a.ni.ah. Prist who played trumpet in the procession that accompanied the Ark of Covenant to Jerusalem in Davids day 1 Ch. 15:3.24.

Sheber.   She.ber. Propably. Fracture. Break down. Crash son of Caleb by Maacah his concubine of the tribe of Judah. 1 Ch. 2:48.

Shebna.h   Propably a short from of Shebaniah an officer of King Hezekiah.

Shecaniah.   Shec.a.ni.ah. Residence of God. Descendant of Aaron whose paternal hose was selected by Lot as 10th of the 24 priestly division that David organized. 1 Ch. 24:1-3.

Shechem.   Che.chem. Sholder of land. Son of Hivite chieftan Hamor Ge. 33:19. Jos. 24:32.

Shechemite.   She.chem.ites. Belong to Shechem. The descendant of Manassah through Shechem. Nu. 26:29.31.

Shedeu.	Shed.e.ur. Propably. Light of the Almighty. Reubenite whose son Elizur was appointed by God to be chieftain of tribe in the wilderness. Nu. 1:5; 2:10.7.30.
She.e.rah.	Mean remain over. Daughter of Ephraim or of his son Beriah.
Shehariah.	Sheharih. Mean. God has looked for head of Benjamite family living in Jerusalem. Son or descendant of Jeroham 1 Ch. 8:1.26-28.
Sheik.	Usually given to the Edomite & Horit tribel chief. The sons of Esau & the son of Seir the Horite Ex. 15:15.
Shekel.	Hebrew unit of weight Isa. 17:5.7. Ez. 4:10 Am 8:5. & of monetary value.
Shelah.	She.lah. Propably. Missile. Son of Arpachshad & grandson of Shm. Who was born in 2333. B.C. & died in 1900 B.C.
Shelanites.	Belonging to Shelah. Family of Judah funded by Shelah. Nu. 26:200.
Sheleph.	The second son of Joktan. Founnder of one of the early post flood family. Ge. 10:26. 1 Ch. 1:20.
Shelesh.	She.lesh. Three parts. Asherite son of Helem head of a family & outstanding warrior. 1 Ch. 7:30.35.
Shelomi.	She.lo.mi. Mean peace Asherite whose chieftain son was appointied to help to help divid the promised land among Israel's tribes Nu. 34.17.18.

Shelomith. Mean peac. Danite daughter of Dibri whose son by Egyptian was put to death in the wilderness for abusing God's name Le. 24:10.14.

Shelomoth. She.lo.moth mean peac. Head of paternal house among descendant of Levis son Gershon 1 Ch. 23:6.7.9.

Shelumiel. She.lu.mi.el. Peace of God. Simeonite. Chieftain. Shelumiel assisted with the nationl census that was taken about a year after the exodus from Egypt. Nu. 1:4.6.2.12.

Shem. Name; fame. One of Noah's three sons; from these all the earth's population spread abroad. Following the global flood Ge. 6:10.9.18.19.

Shema. She.ma. Melodious sound. Son of Hebron & father of Rahamin the line of Judahs descendant through Caleb. Ch. 2:42-44.

Shemariah. Shem.a.ri.ah. Mean God has gurded. Son of King Rehoboam. A great grandson of David 2 Ch. 11:18.19.

Shemeber. Shem.ber. The king of Zeboiim whom Ghedolamer & his allies defeated in low plain of Siddim Ge. 14:1-11.

Shemed. She.med hed of a forefather's house in Benjamin. Son or descendant of Elpael. 1 Ch. 8:1.12.13.

Shemer. She.mer. Mean guard. Descendant of Asher perhaps his great grandson, four sons of Shemr are named. 1 Ch. 7:30-34. Shemer is spelled Shomer in 1 Chronicles. 7:32.

Shiphi.	Shi'phi. Mean abund. Simonite whose son was one of the tribal chieftains who extended their pasture grounds during Hezekiah's reign 1 Ch. 4:24.37-41.
Shiphmite.	Probably belong to Shepham the designation for Zabdi David manager of the wine supply 1 Ch. 27:27.
Shiphtan.	Mean judge. Father of Kemuel the chieftain representing Ephraim when the promised land was divided among the tribes of Israel. Nu. 34:17.18.24.
Shisha.	Father of Solomon's secretaries Elihoreeh & Ahijah. 1 Ki. 4:3.
Shiza.	Shiza. Reubenite father of David warrior Adina 1 Ch. 11:26.42.
Shobab.	Sho.bab. Mean return; bring back. Son of Caleb the brother of Jerahmeel tribe of Judah 1 Ch. 2:9.11.
Sho.Bal.	Horite Sheik. Son of Sair & himself the father of five sons. Ge. 36:20-23. 1 Ch. 1:38.40.
Sho.Bi.	Loyal to King David Shobi & two other brught supplies to David when Absalom rebellion caused the King David & his party to flee Jerusalem. 2 Sa. 17:27-29.
Shomer.	Mean gurd. Descendant of Asher whose four son where chieftains & family head. His name is also spelled Shemer. 1 Ch. 7:30.32.34.40.

Shu'a.   Canaanite father of Judah's wife. Grandfather of Er.onan & Shelah Ge. 38.2-5.12. 1 Ch. 2:3.

Shu.ah.   The sixth. Name of son Abraham by second wife Keturah. 1 Ch. 1:32.

Shu'al.   Fox. Son of Zophah. Headman in the tribe of Asher. 1 Ch. 7:36.40.

Shu.ba.el.   God has taken captive. Desendant of Levi through Moses' son Gershon. 1 Ch. 24:20.26.24.

Shu.hah.   Pit brother of Chelub in the tribe of Judah. 1 Ch. 4:11.

Shu.moth.ites. One of the family of Kiritah - Jearim descendant of Judah through Caleb & Shobal. 1 Ch. 2:19.50.52.

Shu.nam.mit.   Belong to Shunem. Inhabitant of Shunem Abishag the nurs of David in his old age. 1 Ki. 1:34.

Shuni.   Shuni the third Neamed of God seven sons.

Shuphamites.   Benjamite descendant of Shephupham speling of Shuppim & Shephupham. Nu. 26:38.39. 1 Ch. 7:12.

Shuppim.   Descendant of Benjamin propably through Bela & Iri 1 Ch. 7:6.7.12.

Shuthelah.   Son of Ephrim & forfather of tribal family of Shuthelahities. 1 Ch. 7:20. Nu. 26.35-37.

Shuthelahites. Shu.thel.a.hites. Belong to Shuthelah the family descendant of Shuthelah. Nu. 26:35.37.

Sia.   Si.a. Siaha. Si.a.ha. One of Nethinim whose descendant returned from Babylonian exile withe Zerubbabel in 537 B.C. Ezr. 2:1.2.43.

Sib.be.cai.   One of Davids mighty men of Hushathite 1 Ch. 11:26.29. Sibbecai, in a war withe the Philistines at Gob. 2 Sa. 21:18. 1 Ch. 20:4.

Sihon.   Si.hon. Amonit kinge at the time Israel approached the promised land.

Simon.   Mean hear. Listen. Simon Iscariot. Another name for the apostle Peter. Mr. 3:16.

Sinite.   Branch of Canaan's descendant. Ge. 10:15. 1 Ch. 1:15. Sinites settled remains uncertain.

Sippai.   Equivalent name of Saph. A man among those born of Rephaim he was struck down by Sibbecai 1 Ch. 20:4. 2 Sa. 21:18.

Sisera.   Army chief under Canaanite Jabin Sisera.

Sismi.   Descendant of Judah throgh Jerahmeel & Sheshan son of Eleasah & father of Shullam. 1 Ch. 2:3-5; 25.34.40. Sismi possibly lived during the period of the judges.

Sodi. Mean intimate group. Zebulunite whose son Gaddiel spying out the promised land. Nu. 13:2.10.

Sodom. City situated along the south east of Canaan Ge. 10:19.13.32.

Solomon. Mean peace son King David of the line of Judah.

Saint Stephen. Mean grown wreath-the first Christian martyr though his name is Greek he was one of the faithful accepted and followed the Jeuse Chris Messiah. Ac. 7:2.

Sucath.ites. Kenite family of scribes who lived at Jabez 1 Ch. 2:55.

Succoth. Benoth. Deity worshiped by the Babylonian whom the king of Assyria brought into the cities of Samaria after his taking the Israelites of the ten tribe kingdom into exile. 2 Ki. 17:30

Symeon. Sym.e.on. Mean hear listen. Ancestor of Jesus Mother Mary Lu. 3:30. Neam Simon Peter.

Tabbath. After being attacked by Gideon force, the enemy Midianit fled far as outskirts of Abel-meholah by Tabbath. Jg. 7:12.19-22.

Tabrimmon. The Assyrian storm-god. Father of Syrian King Benhadad son of Hezion. 1 Ki. 15:18.

Tahan. Founder of Ephraimite tribal family the Tahanite. Nu. 26:35.

Tahash.   Son of Abraham's brother Nahor by concubine Reumah Ge. 22:23.24.

Tahath.   Mean lower under descendant of Ephraim through Shuthelah 1 Ch. 7:20.

Tahpenes.   Tah.pe.nes. Wife of Egyption pharaoh.

Tahrea.   Son of Micah & descendant of King Saul. 1 Ch. 9:39-41.

Talent.   The largest of Hebrew units of weight & of monetary value. Ex. 38:29. 2 Sa. 12:30.

Talmai.   Brother of Ahiman & Sheshai. Son of Anak. Nu. 13:22. Jas. 15:14 Jg. 1:10.

Tamar.   Palm tree. Daughter in law of Jacob's son Judah.

Taphath.   Daughter of King Solomon & wife of one of his 12 deputies. 1 Ki. 4:7.11.

Tappuah.   Appel tree. One of Hebron's four son's & descendant of Galeb. 1 Ch. 2:42.

Tarea.   Descendant of King Saul through Jonathan also called Tahrea. 1 Ch. 8:33-35.9.39-41.

Tarshish.   Mean shatten. One of Javan four son's. Ge. 10:4.

Tebah.   Te.bah slaughter first named son of Abraham's brother Nahor by his wife concubiane Reumah. Ge. 22:23.24.

Tebaliah.   Good for God a Merarite Levite the third listed son of Hosah. 1 Ch. 26:1.10.11.16.

Telah.   Ephraimite ancestor of Joushua the son of Nun. 1 Ch. 7:20.26-27.

Tema.   One of the son's of Ishmael. Ge. 25:13.15. 1 Ch. 1:29.

Temah.   Forfather of family of Nethinim who returned from Babylon to Jerusalem with Zerubbel Ezr. 2:1.2.43. Ne. 7:55.

Teman.   Right side. South. Descendant of Esau throgh his first born Eliphaz. Ge. 36:10:11. 1 Ch. 1:35.36.

Temani.   Right side. South. Son of Ashhur by his wife Naarah of tribe Judah. 1 Ch. 4:1.5.6.

Thomas.   Aramaic mean twin apostel of Jesus Christ. Was called the twin. Mt. 10:3. Mr. 3:18. Lu. 6:15.

Tibni.   Contender for the kingship of ten tribe kingdom of Israel following the seven day rule of Israel's fifth King Zimriin abut 951. B.C.

Tidal.   The kin gof Goiim and an ally of Elamit King Chedorlaomer.

Tiglath-Pileser. Powerful king of Assyria. Name is also spelled Tilgath pilneser. Mention his name in Bible.

III.

Tillo.   Son Shimon in the tribe of Judah. 1 Ch. 4:20.

Timaeus.   Ti.mae.us. Father of Bartimaeus the blind beggar healed by Jesus Christ. Mr. 10:46.

Timna.   Tim na concubine of Esau's son Eliphaz and mother of Amalek. Ge. 36:10-12. 1 Ch. 1:36.

Timothy.   Tim.o.thy. One who honors God. Son of a Jewess. Eunice, and a Greek father. Ac. 16:1.

Tiras.   Tiras. One of seven sons of Japheth. Ge. 10:2. 1 Ch. 1:5.

Tirhakah.   Tir.ha.kah. Pharaoh Taharga. 2 Ki. 19:8.9.

Tirhah.   Child of Galeb by his concubine Maacah of tribe of Judah 1 Ch. 2:3.48

Tiria.   Son of Jehallelel in the genealogies of Judah. 1 Ch. 4:1.16.

Tirzah.	Tir zah. Mean pleasure approve. One of the five daughter of the Manassite Zelophehad. Nu. 26:29.33.
Toah.	To.ah. Kohathite Levite ancestor of the prophet Samuel and Heman the Singer. 1 Ch. 6:33.34.38.
Tohu.	Ancestor of Samuel. 1 Sa. 1:1. He is apparently called Nahath and Toah in chronical. 1 Ch. 6:16.22-28.34.
Tola.	Grimson. Scarlet cloth. First named son of Issachar who accompanied Jacb household into Egypt in 1728 2 Sa. Ge. 46:8.13.
Togarmah.	To-gar.mah. Son of Gomer the son of Japheth. Great-grandson of Noah. Ge. 10:1-3. 1 Ch. 1:4-6.
Tophel.	Place where Moses addressed the Israelites shortly befor his death. De. 1:1.
Tubal.	Tu.bal. One of the seven sons of Japheth Ge. 10:2 1 Ch. 1:5.
Tubal Cain.	Son of Lamech by his second wife Zillah therfore descendant of Cain an half brother of Jabal and Jubal. He had sister named Naamah Ge. 4:17-22.
Uel.	U.el. One of the sons of Bani who sent away their foreign wife & son's in response to Ezra's counsel Ezr. 10:10.11.34.44.
Ulam.	Father of Bedan of the tribe of Manasseh. 1 Ch. 7:14.16.17.

Ulla.   Asherite whose three sons were tribal family head and valiant warriors 1 Ch. 7:39.40.

Unni.   Un ni. Levite musician who played a stringed instrument in the procession that brought the ark of the covenant to Jerusalem. 1 Ch. 15:3.16.18.20.

Ur.   Light. Father of Eliphal. One of mighty men of David's military forces 1 Ch. 11:26.35. Ur of the Chaldean. The city in Mesopotamia Abram's and brother Haran was born Ge. 11:28. Ac. 7:2.4.

Uri.   Uri. Mean light descendant of Judah through Perez. Herzon. Caleb & Hur. Uri son Bezalel was noted tabernacle craftsman Ex. 31.2.35.30.38.

Uriah.   U.ri.ah. My light is God the Hittite husband of Bath-sheba Uriah was one of David's foreign warriors 2 Sa. 23:39. 1 Ch. 11:41.

Uriel.   U.ri.el. God is light. Levite descendant of Kohath son of Tahth. 1 Ch. 6:22.24.

Uzzia.   Short from of Uzziah. Was an Ashterathite.

Uzziah.   My strength is God. Kohathite Levite son of Uriel 1 Ch. 6:22-24.

Uzziel.   God is strength. Last named of Kohath's four sons. Grandson of Levi. Uncle of Moses and Aaron. Uzziel's three sons. Mishael, Eizaphan and Sithri become head of tribal family in Levi Ex. 6:16.18.20.

Venom.	Poisonous flud seereted by certain snakes Nu. 21.4-9. De. 8:15.
Zaavan.	Za.a.van. Second named son of Horite Sheik Ezer and grandson or descendant of Seir the Horite. Ge. 36:20.21.27. 1 Ch. 1:42.
Zabad.	God has endowed. Ephramite in the family of Shuthelah. 1 Ch. 7:20.21.
Zabbi.	Za.bi. Propably sort from of Zebadiah mean my God endow. Postexilic son of Belai. Among those who terminted their foreign marriage alliances on Ezra's counsel. Ezra. 10:28.44.
Zabbud.	Zab bud. Endowed one of the two leaders of son of Bigvai. A paternal house whose member went to Jerusalem with Ezra in 468 B.C. Ezr. 8:1.14.
Zabdi.	Short from of Zabdiel. Descendant of Judah in the family of Zerahites of Achan Jos. 7:1.17.18.
Zabdiel.	God has endowed. Father of the Jashobeam who was over the first monthly division ministering to King David 1 Ch. 27:2.
Zabud.	Za bud. Endowed. Priestly adviser of King Solomon. Son of Nathan. 1 Ki. 4:5. But Zabud father Nethan my have been prophet. Who close adviser of King David. 2 Sa. 7:3.12.1.
Zaccai.	Zac.cai. Propably short from of Zechariah mean God has remembered. Founder of a family in Israel. Seven hundred and sixty of male descendant returned from the Babylonian exile in 537. B.C. Ezra. 2:1.2.9. Ne. 7;14.

Zaccur.	Zac.cur. Mean remember. Reubenit whose son Shammua was one of 12 spies that Moses sent into the promised land Nu. 13.3.4.
Zadok.	Mean righteous. Zadok was descendant of Aaron through the high priestly line of Eleazar. Ch. 6:3-8.
Zaham.	Loathsome one. Son of King Rehoboam presumably by his wife Mahalath 2 Ch. 11:18.19.23.
Zalaph.	Za.laph father of at least six sons one of whom helped Nehemiah to repair Jerusalem wall. Ne. 3:30.
Zebadiah.	May God endow. Benjamite son or descendant of Beriah. 1 Ch. 8:1.15.16.
Zaza.	Za.za. Son of Janathan. Among the descendant of Jerahmeel in the tribe of Judah. 1 Ch. 2:3-5.
Zebidah.	Mean endow. Wife or concubine of King Joisiah and mothe of King Jehoiakim Zebidah. 2 Ki. 23.34.
Zebulun.	Toleration or possibly. Lofty abde. Habitation the sixth son of Jacob's wife Leah.
Zechariah.	God has rememberd. One of the ten sons of Jeiel in the tribe of Benjamin. 1 Ch. 9:35-37.

Zecher.	Shortend from of Zechariah. Descendant of Jeiel the father of Gibeon. 1 Ch. 8:29-31.
Zedekiah.	God is righteousness son of Chenaanah false prophet who assured King Ahab.
Zeeb.	Wolf. Prince of Midian in the force that Gideon & Israelites defeated after their inital loss.
Zelek.	Ammonit warrior who joined David mithy men of the military forces 1 Ch. 11:26.39. 2 Sa. 23:37.
Zemirah.	Ze.mi.rah. Mean melody. Family head in the tribe of Benjamin. Son or descendant of Becher. 1 Ch. 7:6.8.9.
Zephaniah.	God has concealed treasured up. Levite in the genealogical line from Kohath to Samuel and Heman. 1 Ch. 6:33-38.
Zelek.	Ammonite warrior who joined David's mighty men of the military forces 1 Ch. 11:26.39.
Zelophehad.	Mean possbly shadow. Shelter from dread descendant of Manasseh through Machir.
Zemarite.	Family or tribe that descendant from Ham son Canaan Ge. 10.15.18; 1 Ch. 1:13.16.

Zephaniah.	God has concealed treasured up. Levite in the genealogical line from Kohth to Samuel & Heman 1 Ch. 6:33-38.
Zepho.	Third son name of Eliphaz grandson of Esau and Sheik of Edomite tribe Ge. 36:10.11.15. 1 Ch. 1:36.
Zephon.	First name son of God and founder of family of Zephonite also called Ziphon Ge. 46:16. Nu. 26:15.
Zephonites.	Belong to Zephon. Family descendant from God through Zebon. Ge. 46:16. Nu. 26:15.
Zerah.	Propably short from of Zerahiah. An Edomite Sheik. Zerah was son of Reuel and grandson of Esau & Basemath. Ishmael's daughter Ge. 36:3.4.13.17. 1 Ch. 1:37.
Zerahiah.	God has flased. Descendant of Aaron through Eleazar and Phinehas in the high-priestly line 1 Ch. 6:3.4.6.
Zerahites.	Belong to Zerh. Descendant of Simon's son Zerh. Nu. 26:12.13.
Zeresh.	Ze.resh. Wife of Haman.
Zereth.	Ze.reth first named son Helah bore to Asshur of tribe of Judah. 1 Ch. 4:1.5.7.
Zeri.	Ze ri. One of Jeduthun's six sons. All of whom were temple musician's. 1 Ch. 25:1.3.

Zeror.	Ze ror. Mean flint. Ancestor of King Saul. Listed as son of Becorath and father of Abiel of the tribe of Benjamin 1 Sa. 9:1.
Zeruah.	Ze.ru.ah. Mean. Beleprous mother of King Jeroboam.
Zerubbabel.	From Akkadian mean seed offspring of Babel. First governor of the repatriated Jews.
Zeruiah.	Mean balsam King David's sister or half sister and mother of Joab. Abishai & Asahel Zeruiah's sister Abigail. 2 Sa. 17:25.
Zetham.	Ze tham. Propably mean. Olive. Olive tree. Gershonite Levite descendant from Ladan. 1 Ch. 23:7-9.26.
Zethan.	Mean olive. Olive tree. Descendant of Benjamine through Jediael and Bilan 1 Ch. 7:6.10.
Zia.	Z.ia. Mean tremble quake, violently shake. Gadite who lived in Bashan. 1 Ch. 5:7.13.
Zibia.	Zib.i.a. Gazelle family head in the tribe of Benjamin son of Shahraim by his wife Hodesh 1 Ch. 8:1.8-10.
Zibiah.	Zib.i.ah. Female Gazelle. Mother of King Jehoash of
Zichri.	Short from Zechariah mean God has remembered. Third named son of Izhar. Grandson of Kohth, a Levite Ex. 6:18.21.

Ziha.   First listed family of Nethinim who accompaied the exiled Israelites back to
               Judah in 537 B.C. Ezr. 2:1.2.43. Ne 7:46.

Zillah.   Zil.lah. Shadow. Shelter. One of the two wives of Lamech.

Zillethai.   Maen shadow shelter. Head of family of Benjmites that lived in Jerusaleme.
               Son of Shimei. 1 Ch. 8:1:20.21.

Zilpah.   Leah's maidservant & one of Jacob's secondary wives.

Zimmah.   Gershonite Levite. 1 Ch. 6:20.

Zimran.   First named of the six son's Keturah to Abraham. Zimran. Ge. 25:1.2.6. 1 Ch.
               1:32.

Zimri.   Son of Zeroh and grandson of Judah. 1 Ch. 2:4.6.

Zina.   Zin a. Descendant of gershon through Shimei 1 Ch. 23:6.7.10. He is called Zizah
               in chronical. 11.

Ziphah.   Son of Jehallelel in the tribe of Judah. 1 Ch. 4:1.16.

Zippor.   Zip.por. Bird father of Moab's King Balak Nu. 22:2.4.10.16.23.18 Jos. 24:9. Jg.
               11:25.

Zipporah.	Zip.po.rah. Bird or small bird the wife of Moses. Zipporah met Moses at well.
Ziza.	Son of King Rehoboam by Absalom's granddaughter Maacah when the royal successio was directed to Ziza's. Brother Abijah. 2 Ch. 11:20.22.23.
Zizah.	Second listed son of Shimei head of a paternal house of Gershonite Levites. 1 Ch. 23:6.7.10.
Zobebah.	Zo.be.bah. Descendant of Koz in the tribe of Judah. 1 Ch. 4:1.8.
Zohar.	??? Zohar. Hittite whose son Ephron sold the cave of Machpelah to Abraham. Ge. 23:7-9.25.9.
Zoheth.	Zo.heth. Descendant of Ishi in the tribe of Judah 1 Ch. 4:1.20.
Zophah.	Leading member of the tribe of Asher. Elevent sons of his are listed 1 Ch. 7:35-37.40.
Zophai.	Zo.phai. Propably mean honeycomb. Son of certain Elkanah & ancestor of Samuel. 1 Ch. 6:26.28.33-35.
Zorathites.	Belong to Zorah descendant of Shobal of the tribe of Judah 1 Ch. 2:3.52.53.42
Zorites.	Belong to Zorah descendant of Salma of the tribe of Judah. 1 Ch. 2:3.54.

Zuar.	Zu ar. Be insignificant man of Issachar whose son Nethanel was tribal chieftain in the wildrnes Nu. 1:8.16.25.
Zuph.	Honeycomb. Kohathite & ancestor of Samuel.
Zur.	Rock. On of the five kings of Midian at the time Israel approached the promised land. Nu. 25;14-18-31.1.27.8. Jas. 13:21.
Zuriel.	Zu.ri.el. My rock is God. Wilderness. Chieftain of Merarite Levites son of Abihil Nu. 3:35.
Zurishaddai.	Zu.ri.shad.dai. May rock is the Almighty. Simeonite whose son Shelumiel was tribal chieftain during the wilderness journey. Nu. 1:6.16.2.2.12.7:36.41.10.19.
Zuzim.	Zu.zim. People east of the Jordan River whom Chedorlaomar forces defeated in Ham. Ge. 14:5.

JOSEPH BAHRIBEK

Printed in the United States
by Baker & Taylor Publisher Services